P9-AFP-597

ROOMS IN THE DARWIN HOTEL

ROOMS IN THE DARWIN HOTEL

STUDIES IN ENGLISH LITERARY CRITICISM AND IDEAS 1880-1920

TOM GIBBONS

UNIVERSITY OF WESTERN AUSTRALIA PRESS

First published in 1973 by the
University of Western Australia Press, Nedlands, W.A. 6009

Agents: Eastern States of Australia, New Zealand, Papua and New Guinea:
Melbourne University Press; United Kingdom, Europe, Middle East, and
the Caribbean: Angus & Robertson (U.K.) Ltd, London; Singapore, Thailand,
Malaysia, Indonesia, Hong Kong, Philippines: Angus & Robertson (S.E. Asia)
Pty Ltd, Singapore; United States, its territories and possessions, and Canada:
International Scholarly Book Services Inc., Portland, Oregon

Printed in Australia by Frank Daniels Pty Ltd, Perth, Western Australia, and
bound by Stanley Owen and Sons Pty Ltd, Alexandria, New South Wales

Registered in Australia for transmission by post as a book

© Tom Gibbons 1973

Library of Congress catalog card number 73-83715
ISBN 0 85564 072 3

Published with the assistance of a grant from the Australian Academy of
the Humanities

Contents

Preface

In this book I make amends for the neglect which has largely overtaken the literary criticism of three prominent figures of the period 1880-1920: Havelock Ellis, who is best known for his pioneering work in the field of sexual psychology, Arthur Symons, who is generally and quite unfairly thought of as the author of a handful of Decadent poems, and Alfred Orage, who is mainly remembered as editor from 1907 until 1922 of the influential political and literary magazine *The New Age*.

While there are important ways in which Ellis, Symons and Orage differ as critics, there are equally important ways in which they have much in common with each other. In discussing their criticism I draw particular attention to certain beliefs, attitudes and concerns which they have in common with each other and with many of their contemporaries, as these seem central to our understanding of a complex, fascinating and seminal literary period which continues to elude definition. The most important of these beliefs are: religiously, a belief in some form of mysticism; politically, a belief in the desirability of an élite social class; aesthetically, a strong leaning towards transcendental and anti-naturalistic theories of art and literature.

In my first chapter I show how ideas and beliefs of this kind were nourished by the evolutionary notions which dominated the thinking of the period 1880-1920. I also draw attention to the way in which these same notions, whilst encouraging the mood of millennial optimism in which Ellis, Symons and Orage wrote, at the same time exacerbated public alarm about the dangers of social and literary degeneration and decadence. In my final chapter, having argued that orthodox twentieth-century modernism is deeply indebted to the occult symbolist aesthetic which flourished in the evolutionary climate of this earlier period, I offer my own views on the more important of the general issues which my survey appears to raise for students of literature and literary history.

Although my study is mainly concerned with certain relationships between ideas and literary criticism during the period 1880-1920, I hope that it will throw a useful light upon important aspects of the period's creative literature, which I assume to be major by any standard. It should help to 'place', for example, the evolutionism of George Bernard Shaw's *Man and Superman* (1903), the pervasive imagery of cancerous social 'disorder' in H. G. Wells's *Tono-Bungay* (1909), the ironic use of Lombroso's notions of individual degeneracy in Joseph Conrad's *The Secret Agent* (1907), and even the 'psychic apparitions' which so fascinated Henry James and which dominate *The Turn of the Screw* (1898). More generally, and perhaps more importantly, it should help to establish that the élitism and occultism of W. B. Yeats were the reverse of unusual during the period under discussion.

As Ellis, Symons and Orage and their criticism are not well known, I have tried to bring them closer to the reader by including short outlines of their lives. For the biographical information contained in these outlines I am indebted almost entirely to the following standard biographies: *Havelock Ellis: Philosopher of Love* by Houston Peterson, *Arthur Symons: A Critical Biography* by Roger Lhombreaud, and *A. R. Orage: A Memoir* by Philip Mairet.

I have also tried to bring Ellis, Symons and Orage closer to the reader by quoting their own words as often as possible. In quoting from Havelock Ellis I have been able to rely nearly always upon his books of collected essays. Exactly the reverse is true of Symons and Orage. In quoting from their criticism I have returned wherever possible to their original articles as published in periodicals. In the case of Orage this was necessary because most of his criticism is uncollected, such collections as exist being more misleading than other-wise. In the case of Symons it was necessary because his own collections of essays, though reasonably complete and repre-sentative, give almost no indication of the interesting and rapid chronological development of his critical ideas.

The 'Darwin Hotel' of my title stands for the structure of evolutionary assumptions which dominated Western thought between 1880 and 1920. I have adapted it from the fictional hotel of that name described in the opening pages of *Caesar's Column,* a prophetic novel about the late twen-tieth century which was first published under a pseudonym in 1890 by Ignatius Donnelly, better known as a contender for Bacon's authorship of Shakespeare's plays. According to Donnelly, the cut-throat capitalism of his day is heading towards a world controlled by a ruthless oligarchy of inter-national financiers, in which the great majority of people will have been reduced to serfdom. The characteristics of the upper-class diners in New York's palatial Darwin Hotel of 1988, so named 'in honour of the great English philoso-pher of the last century', are intended by Donnelly as a warning of what will happen if the Darwinian law of the survival of the fittest is accepted as the sole criterion of human progress:

> . . . I could not help noticing that the women, young and old, were much alike in some particulars, as if some general causes had moulded them into the same form. . . . Their looks were bold, penetrating, immodest, if I may so express it, almost to fierceness . . .
>
> The chief features in the expression of the men were incredulity, unbelief, cunning, observation, heartlessness.

The titles of most other works consulted have been in-corporated into the necessarily extensive references to each chapter. This seemed preferable to overloading a short book still further by providing a separate bibliography. The in-terested reader may however also be referred to *The Critic's*

Alchemy (1953) by Ruth Z. Temple, who discusses Arthur Symons and other critics who introduced French symbolism into England, to *'The New Age' under Orage* (1967) by Wallace Martin, who describes Orage's editorship of that legendary periodical, and to *Nietzsche in England 1880-1914* (1970) by David S. Thatcher, who considers Orage as an important interpreter of Nietzsche's work to English readers.

A useful survey of the occult background to symbolism in literature is provided in *The Way Down and Out* (1959) by John Senior. The occult background to symbolism in painting is described in *Dreamers of Decadence* by Philippe Jullian (English translation 1971).

                                                        T.H.G.

Acknowledgements

Some of the material in some of these studies derives from a doctoral dissertation approved by the University of Cambridge in 1966 and entitled 'Literary Criticism and the Intellectual Milieu: some aspects of the period 1880-1914'. Whilst at Cambridge during 1964 and 1965 it was my privilege to work under Professors John Holloway and Graham Hough, whose advice and encouragement I here take pleasure in acknowledging. I am also very much indebted to colleagues in the University of Western Australia who have read and commented upon the various drafts of these studies, to the Haags Gemeentemuseum for permission to reproduce the Mondrian *Evolution* triptych on the dust-jacket, to the Australian Academy of the Humanities for a grant towards costs of publication, and to the editors of *The British Journal of Aesthetics* and *Renaissance and Modern Studies* for permission to reprint material on Symons and Ellis respectively. Special thanks are also due to staff of the Reid Library of the University of Western Australia for cheerfully locating and acquiring seemingly inexhaustible amounts of Symons material on my behalf.

1

The Age of Evolutionism

Looked at in the very broadest possible way, the period 1880-1920 was one of full-scale ideological reaction from the scientific materialism, atheism, determinism and pessimism of the mid-nineteenth century. During the last quarter of the nineteenth century these gave way on many sides to their opposites: philosophical idealism, religious transcendentalism, vitalism and optimism. In the words of a central figure of the period, the mystico-socialist poet Edward Carpenter, the early 1880s saw 'the inception of a number of new movements or enterprises tending towards the establishment of mystical ideas and a new social order'. In the years 1881 and 1882:

> quite a number of societies were started with objects of the kind indicated. Hyndman's Democratic Federation, Edmund Gurney's Society for Psychical Research, Mme. Blavatsky's Theosophical Society . . . and many other associations of the same kind marked the coming of a great reaction from the smug commercialism and materialism of the mid-Victorian epoch, and a preparation for the new universe of the twentieth century.[1]

The 'great reaction' described by Carpenter derived so much of its strength from current notions of 'evolution' that, to follow a lead given by Bertrand Russell, the period as a whole might conveniently if inelegantly be named the Age of Evolutionism. Towards the end of the period which begins with the movements described by Edward Carpenter, Bertrand Russell wrote as follows:

> Evolutionism, in one form or another, is the prevailing creed of our time. It dominates our politics, our literature, and not least our philosophy. Nietzsche, pragmatism, Bergson, are phases in its philosophic development, and their popularity far beyond the circles of professional philosophers shows its consonance with the spirit of the age.[2]

Such all-embracing tags as the 'Age of Evolutionism' have obvious dangers, from which the very notion of a literary period is itself of course not free. Used with care, however, they can helpfully remind us of the assumptions and the preoccupations which distinguish one age from another. At present the period 1880-1920 is most frequently referred to by literary historians as the 'transition' period between Victorian and modern literature, which is both noncommittal and in the end patronizing. The term 'Age of Evolutionism' not only gives the period a definite status and character of its own, but as far as the general development of art and literature during the period is concerned, it helps to make sense of two of the outstanding features of the years during which Ellis, Symons and Orage were writing.

The first of these was the rise of symbolism during the 1890s. Symbolism, which was originally an occult or supernatural theory of art and literature, strove to replace the pseudo-scientific theories of art and literature known as naturalism and impressionism. Turning their backs upon the physical world which the naturalists had sought to describe as accurately as possible, the symbolists sought to communicate spiritual realities with an equal degree of accuracy.

The second outstanding feature of the period was a radical change of tone in the early years of the new century, which marked the transition from symbolism to expressionism. The anti-naturalistic doctrines of the symbolists continued to hold sway, but were proclaimed in an increasingly violent and forceful manner, as for example in the magazine *BLAST,* which was published in 1914 and 1915 by the

English abstract painter Wyndham Lewis and his vorticist colleagues, who included the poet Ezra Pound.

Both of these major developments were closely connected with the spread of evolutionary thinking during the period 1880-1920. Evolutionism greatly encouraged the revival of those occult and mystical doctrines which underlay symbolism and expressionism and which sharply distinguish them from the preceding movements of naturalism and impressionism. The violence and the acclamation of energy which characterized expressionism also owed much to the influence of such evolutionist philosophers as Nietzsche and Bergson, as did the increasing violence of English and European political life between 1905 and 1914. Important intermediaries for their ideas were the French syndicalist philosopher Georges Sorel, author of *Réflexions sur la Violence* (1908), and the Italian artist-militarist-superman Gabriele D'Annunzio.

The term 'Age of Evolutionism' is apt for a number of other reasons. For example, it covers the period's obsession with 'decadence', an obsession which cannot be fully understood without reference to the framework of evolutionary thought, and which can easily distort our own view of what was actually happening to literature and the arts between 1880 and 1914. It is also apt because much of the period's literature, as well as its criticism, is permeated with evolutionary notions. The novels of Thomas Hardy, the poetry of John Davidson and the plays of George Bernard Shaw, like the criticism of John Addington Symonds and Max Nordau (the influential author of *Degeneration*), are all heavily indebted to evolutionary thinking. The same is true of the many popular and often apocalyptic novels which were written during the period about the future of mankind.[3]

The term 'Age of Evolutionism' seems equally apt when we consider the strange new style which came to dominate the decorative arts of the period, the style of *art nouveau*. In his book on this movement, drawing attention to the influence of Darwinism on late-nineteenth-century 'biological

Romanticism',[4] Robert Schmutzler claims with some justi-
fication that all the 'swinging, swirling, throbbing, sprouting,
and blossoming' which characterizes the style of *art nouveau*
is 'intended to be an unequivocal sign of organic life'.[5]

Schmutzler seems equally justified when he speaks of a
new romanticism emerging towards the end of the nineteenth
century, for the general state of European thought at that
time had important things in common with that of a century
before. According to M. H. Abrams's account of the original
romantic movement, the publication of J. G. Herder's essay
'On the Knowing and Feeling of the Human Soul' in Germany in 1778 heralds a new and revolutionary 'age of biologism'. In this, 'the area of the most exciting and seminal
discoveries having shifted from physical science to the science
of life, biology has begun to replace Cartesian and Newtonian
mechanics as the great source of concepts which, migrating
into other provinces, were modifying the general character
of ideation'.[6] The ultimate effects of Darwin's *On the Origin
of Species* were to be remarkably similar. Despite the profound dismay which it caused during the years immediately
following its publication, it in fact inaugurated a second and
equally radical 'age of biologism', in which world-views based
upon evolutionary biology largely superseded those underwritten by the mechanistic physical sciences of the High
Victorian period, thus giving a powerful new impetus to
romantic philosophy and aesthetics.

By 'evolutionism' is meant the highly questionable employ-
ment of biological theories of natural selection, which Darwin himself never stated in any clear or final form, in realms
of thought unconnected with biology. The first thorough-
going evolutionist, and probably the most influential systematic philosopher of the second half of the nineteenth
century, was Herbert Spencer, to whom we owe the phrase
'the survival of the fittest'. As early as 1862 Spencer had
detected in all terrestrial and cosmic processes throughout
history the operations of a single 'law' of evolution: 'the
transformation of the homogeneous into the heterogeneous',[7]

or, in other words, of whatever is undifferentiated and indistinct into whatever is more distinct and individual. Since Spencer himself reserved the right to decide what should be categorized as homogeneous and what as heterogeneous, it is hardly surprising that his law was invariably validated by whatever process he chose to describe.

Spencer's system gave an appearance of unity and uniformity to the boundless diversity of phenomena by presenting the whole of existence, past, present and future, as a single consistent process. Other and later evolutionists achieved similar results by boldly hypostatizing such supposed cosmic evolutionary processes into a single, all-pervading, all-controlling evolutionary will, life force, or *élan vital*. The notion that the universe was pervaded by this all-powerful and purposive evolutionary force gave a new and powerful impetus to a variety of religious philosophies based upon the doctrine that God is immanent in or permeates the whole of creation, and such venerable pantheistic religious philosophies as Brahmanism and Neo-Platonism now received the apparent support of the most up-to-date scientific thought. A good deal of later thinking along these lines was anticipated by Edward Carpenter when, in an extremely *avant-garde* manuscript dating from about 1870, he identified the evolutionary process with spiritual progress towards union with a Brahmanistic cosmic mind: 'So each mind grows towards the divine mind', he wrote. 'And this, as we view it externally in Nature, is the Law of Evolution.'[8] Christian theologians, similarly, could call upon evolutionary science in support of the doctrine of immanence. By 1889, for example, the Reverend Aubrey Moore could perceive in Darwinism a providential reminder of God's immanence in nature:

It seems as if, in the providence of God, the mission of modern science was to bring home to our unmetaphysical ways of thinking the great truth of the Divine immanence in creation, which is not less essential to the Christian idea of God than to a philosophical view of nature. And it comes to us almost like a new truth, which we cannot at once fit in with the old.[9]

Writing in *Lux Mundi,* an extremely important collection of theological essays edited by Bishop Charles Gore, Moore provides a striking example of the way in which evolutionary ideas which had seemed at first to threaten the very foundations of Christianity were soon to be adduced as crucial evidence *in favour of* Christianity. The 'new truth' of evolution was in fact very rapidly fitted in with the old, and by no means in the field of Christian apologetics alone. It could be invoked on any side of any question, and was pressed into the service of any and every set of beliefs. Much that is at first sight puzzling in speculative thought after 1880 becomes clearer when we realize that vague and often conflicting notions about evolution are being used to give an up-to-date and 'scientific' air to beliefs which were venerable before Darwin or Spencer had published a word.

The Age of Evolutionism was not the age of a new ideology, broadly speaking, but of old ideologies rehabilitated. They were rehabilitated both directly, by the introduction of evolutionary diction, imagery and assumptions into public discourse, and indirectly as a result of a new and favourable climate of opinion. This important paradox of the period is memorably summed up in Orage's contention that evolution is in fact proceeding *backwards.* 'Evolution (in which I firmly believe) ', he wrote in 1915, 'connotes in this age, not the multiplication and outspread of human faculties, but their reduction by assimilation and intensification.' Formerly, he goes on to say:

> the race sought properly the *mouths* of the streams of life. Since the Christian era, at any rate, the word of progress is to seek their sources. . . . Our route homeward is therefore via the eighteenth century back to the seventeenth, and thence, if we are fortunate, to the still earlier centuries of our golden race.[10]

In other words, as he put the matter still more succinctly a few months later, 'To go back is to go forward.'[11] The same paradox was later to be neatly encapsulated in the title of one of George Bernard Shaw's most famous plays, which advises us that evolutionary progress is to be achieved only by going *Back to Methuselah.*

Mystical and occult doctrines, in particular, gained a new lease of life as a result of the spread of evolutionistic thinking during the late nineteenth century. The revival of these doctrines, which appear to underlie the type of visionary aesthetic subscribed to in different degrees by Ellis, Symons and Orage, is described in the first of the two main sections which complete the present introductory chapter. In the first of these sections I draw particular attention to developments in academic philosophy and theology during the late nineteenth century, to the more popular and widespread interest in spiritualism and Theosophy, and to the influence of two authors so ostensibly unalike as Bulwer Lytton and Arthur Schopenhauer. In the second section I describe some of the ways in which evolutionistic thinking gave new and often alarming currency to certain traditional notions about literature, society, and the relationships between the two.

ii

Like the German-inspired romanticism of a century before, late-nineteenth-century romanticism was in its broadest sense 'a retort to [materialistic] scientism, a program for poetic re-establishment of the analytically dissolved harmony between man and nature and between the parts of man's own consciousness'.[12] Its message was profoundly attractive to many whose sense of the significance and ultimate harmony of human experience had been shattered by the materialist-monism and determinism of mid-Victorian science, by the 'higher criticism' of the Bible, and by mid-nineteenth-century advances in geology and astronomy.

The widespread religious despair brought about by these developments is of course well known. What is perhaps less well known, however, and what makes subsequent reactions in the direction of vitalism and occultism more readily comprehensible, is the type of High Victorian pseudo-scientific writing upon which this despair fed, and of which David Strauss's mechanistic description of the universe provides us with so lurid an example. David Strauss (1808-74), the German theologian and biographer, is best known for his rationalistic *The Life of Jesus,* which was translated into English by George Eliot in 1846. In his enormously popular book *The Old Faith and the New,* which was translated into English in 1873, he depicts the universe not merely as a machine but as a massive instrument of torture:

> In the enormous machine of the universe, amid the incessant whirl and hiss of its jagged iron wheels, amid the deafening crash of its ponderous stamps and hammers, in the midst of this whole terrific commotion, man, a helpless and defenceless creature, finds himself placed, not secure for a moment that on an imprudent motion a wheel may not seize and rend him, or a hammer crush him to powder.

The central image here appears to be that of a mechanical drop-forge or steam-hammer, while such words as 'jagged', 'seize and rend', and 'crush' suggest the torture-chamber and the punishments of the damned. According to Strauss, who speaks not in the least ironically, we have however the grand consolation of knowing that the operations of this 'world-machine' are so completely determined that instant and universal destruction would be caused by the slightest variation in any one of them:

> We do not only find the revolution of pitiless wheels in our world-machine, but also the shedding of soothing oil. Our God . . . unseals the well-springs of consolation within our own bosoms. . . . He teaches us to perceive

that to demand an exception in the accomplishment of a single natural law, would be to demand the destruction of the universe.[13]

'I well remember', writes Havelock Ellis understandably, concerning the unsatisfied religious longings of his adolescence, 'the painful feelings with which I read . . . *The Old Faith and the New*. . . . I had to acknowledge to myself that the scientific principles of the universe as Strauss laid them down presented, so far as I knew, the utmost scope in which the human spirit could move. But what a poor scope!'[14] Ellis had lost the evangelical faith of his childhood, but in late adolescence underwent a conversion to a type of religious vitalism as a result of reading *Life in Nature* (1862) by James Hinton (1822-75), the Victorian surgeon, philosophical writer and sexual reformer. Although Hinton saw the universe as an orderly mechanism, as Strauss did, writes Ellis, he also saw it as very much more:

> As he viewed it, the mechanism was not the mechanism of a factory, it was vital, with all the glow and warmth and beauty of life; it was, therefore, something which not only the intellect might accept, but the heart might cling to. The bearing of this conception on my state of mind is obvious. It acted with the swiftness of an electric contact; the dull aching tension was removed; the two opposing psychic tendencies were fused in delicious harmony, and my whole attitude towards the universe was changed. It was no longer an attitude of hostility and dread, but of confidence and love. My self was at one with the Not-Self, my will one with the universal will. I seemed to walk in light; my feet scarcely touched the ground; I had entered a new world.[15]

Ellis here adds weight to Stephen Toulmin's claim, extremely relevant in any discussion of the Age of Evolutionism, that world-views derived from biology tend to be highly optimistic, while those derived from physics tend to be quite

the reverse.[16] As a result of the experience which he describes, Ellis achieved the unity for which he longed. He not
only unified the opposing tendencies within his own psyche,
but simultaneously became at one with nature. Large numbers of his contemporaries were to find in various forms of
mysticism and occultism the psychic integration and the
unified view of human experience which they so desperately
sought, and which orthodox Christianity no longer seemed
able to provide.

The 1890s saw the culmination of a transcendentalist revival which had been gathering force since about 1875. By
1894, for example, in his widely read *Social Evolution,* the
once-famous British sociologist Benjamin Kidd (1858-1916)
could claim that agnosticism was *passé*, 'belonging to a phase
of thought beyond which the present generation feels itself
. . . to have moved'.[17] Indeed, he proceeds to argue that
religious belief must be fostered at all costs, on the novel
grounds that evolutionary progress is impossible without it.
A major element of this general revival of transcendentalism
was a revival of various types of mysticism and occult idealism, and the entries under 'Occult Science' and 'Theosophy'
in *The British Museum Subject Index, 1881-1900* amply
support the claim made in the mid-nineties by the well-
known Theosophical writer and editor G. R. S. Mead (1863-
1933) that the demand for books on Neo-Platonism and
other forms of mysticism was at that time steadily increasing.[18]

'Occultism' is a difficult term to define. It denotes a large
variety of different beliefs and practices such as fortune-
telling, spiritualism, magic, witchcraft, necromancy and alchemy, and it has inevitably acquired adverse connotations
of fraud and deception. The word itself, according to Murray's *New English Dictionary,* was unknown until the out-
set of the period which concerns us, being used for the first
time in 1881 by the leading Theosophical writer A. P. Sinnett, shortly to be quoted in these pages.

What appears to be common to all occult doctrines is a belief that the universe is essentially spiritual, so that to this extent occultism generally may be described as a form of idealism. Two of the most recurrent notions of the many 'occult philosophers' are essentially Neo-Platonic: they are (a) that the life or energy of God permeates all created things, visible and invisible, and (b) that earthly phenomena 'correspond' to, i.e. are symbols or counterparts of, spiritual realities. These Neo-Platonic doctrines are immediately recognizable in a passage from the French poet Gérard de Nerval which is quoted by Arthur Symons in *The Symbolist Movement in Literature*:

> All things live, all things are in motion, all things correspond; the magnetic rays emanating from myself or others traverse without obstacle the infinite chain of created things: a transparent network covers the world, whose loose threads communicate more and more closely with the planets and the stars. Now a captive upon the earth, I hold converse with the starry choir, which is feelingly a part of my joys and sorrows.[19]

In its hypothetically purest form, and for the purposes of this study, occultism is perhaps best regarded as a continuation of the Neo-Platonic tradition, according to which the universe is living, spiritual, and unified. Such a view, which is directly opposed to the High Victorian scientistic view of the universe as dead, material, and atomistic, could hardly fail to have been encouraged by the late-nineteenth-century concept of evolution as an all-pervading life force. Nor is this surprising. One of the commonest occult notions is what Arthur Symons describes as 'an eternal, minute, intricate, almost invisible life, which runs through the whole universe'.[20] There is little to choose between Symons's 'invisible life', which the alchemist 'Paracelsus' (1493-1541) had earlier called the *fluidium,* and what Henri Bergson, the philosopher of creative evolution, called the *élan vital.*

The tone for the late-nineteenth-century revival of transcendentalism in England was set by the universities, and
especially by the University of Oxford, where the old orthodoxy of native empiricism finally yielded to the new orthodoxy of German metaphysical idealism on the eve of the
period under discussion. The Neo-Hegelian movement as
such began in the 1870s with T. H. Green's *Introductions to
Hume's Treatise of Human Nature* (1874) and Edward
Caird's *A Critical Account of the Philosophy of Kant* (1877).
The manifesto of the movement, the *Essays in Philosophical
Criticism* edited by Seth and Haldane, was published in
1883, and the movement reached its zenith in the absolute
idealism of Bernard Bosanquet and F. H. Bradley (*Appearance and Reality,* 1893).

Among T. H. Green's most enthusiastic followers at Oxford were the young high-church clergymen such as Charles
Gore and Henry Scott-Holland who were to produce in
1889 the extremely influential *Lux Mundi: Studies in the
Religion of the Incarnation.* Although its attempt to reconcile Christianity with science dismayed the older members
of the Oxford Movement, this important collection of essays
marks a further strengthening of the anglo-catholic faction
within the Church of England, which had steadily been gain-
ing ground at the expense of the low-church party. The year
of *Lux Mundi,* it is relevant to note here, also saw the last
of the prosecutions of ritualists which had attended the progress of the Oxford Movement since its inception.

The marked shift towards anglo-catholicism in the Church
of England during the last quarter of the nineteenth century
had two major causes. Firstly, the doubts cast by biblical
criticism on the literal interpretation of the scriptures had
led to an increasing emphasis on the mystical and sacramental aspects of Christianity. Secondly, such important
studies in comparative religion as Sir James Frazer's *The
Golden Bough* (1890) led to a renewed emphasis on the
Eucharist as the central act of Christian worship. In his
History of the English People the French historian Elie

Halévy writes as follows: 'Christian faith might be emperilled [sic] by the discovery that the doctrine of the Real Presence of God in . . . the Eucharist represented a survival of primitive religion.' Nevertheless, this discovery

> proved that the doctrine was not an excrescence on the body of Christian doctrine, for which the Catholic Church was responsible. . . . In short, the conclusions of Robertson Smith and Fraser [sic] favoured a revival of Catholic 'sacramentalism' at the expense of 'Evangelical Protestantism'. Fraser's [sic] work had scarcely appeared before the Anglo-Catholic theologians of the High Church party combined its theories with the Hegelian philosophy which was current at Oxford . . .[21]

The 1890s as a whole saw an increasing number of conversions to Roman Catholicism, and the end of the century witnessed the beginning of a strong revival of interest in mysticism within the Church of England. In 1899 W. R. Inge, later to be Dean of St Paul's, published his influential Bampton lectures on *Christian Mysticism*. In the same year appeared *The Symbolist Movement in Literature*, in which Arthur Symons made public his own conversion to mysticism.

Spiritualism as an organized movement derives from the late eighteenth century. Its doctrines were based upon those of the famous Swedish visionary Emanuel Swedenborg (1688-1772), and its practices upon the techniques for inducing hypnotic trance discovered by Friedrich Anton Mesmer (1734-1815). At the meetings of the numerous mesmeric societies which sprang up in France during the late eighteenth century, attempts to cure the sick were made at séances held in darkened rooms, the mesmerized patients joining hands to form 'magnetic circles'. The early-nineteenth-century German Magnetists, who regarded the hypnotic trance as a means of communicating with the world of spirits, and of whom the most prominent was the writer and physician 'Jung-Stilling' (Johann Heinrich Jung, 1740-1817), turned these mesmeric practices into a highly efficient means of disseminating Swedenborgian doctrines. By 1840 their apocalyptic mixture of mesmerism and Swedenborgian 'spiritism' had reached the United States of America, where Andrew Jackson Davies, known as the 'Poughkeepsie seer', became the most famous of its early spokesmen.

It was in 1848 that there occurred in the American township of Arcadia the famous 'mysterious rappings' which were to convert the already powerful movement of 'spiritism' into a world-wide force. Employing an alphabetical code of raps (for Samuel Morse and his invention were much in the news at that time), the young daughters of a certain John D. Fox amazed their elders by establishing communication with the 'spirit' whose noises had been disturbing the household. The Fox daughters (who appear to have produced the 'spirit-rappings' themselves, by manipulating their knee and ankle joints) went on to become the first professional spiritualist 'mediums'. Within a year New York City alone had a hundred such mediums, and numerous periodicals such as *The Spiritual Telegraph* sprang up to propagate the doctrines of Swedenborgian spiritism and the newly discovered technique for communicating with the spirits themselves.

These ideas and practices quickly found their way to Europe, and by 1860 séances, mediums and spiritualist books and periodicals were as common in England as in America. The twenty years between 1860 and 1880 constitute what Frank Podmore in his *Modern Spiritualism* calls 'the classic period of English Spiritualism'.[22] Tennyson and Rossetti attended séances during the 1860s, while the famous American medium Daniel Dunglas Home made fictional appearances as 'Margrave' in Lytton's *A Strange Story* (1861-62) and as 'Mr Sludge' in Browning's *Dramatis Personae* (1864).

In 1870 the respectability of the spiritualist movement in England was considerably enhanced by the favourable report made upon it by the distinguished London Dialectical Society, and when the Society for Psychical Research was founded in 1882 spiritualism became the subject of serious scientific investigation and philosophical conjecture. In the

words of the Society's first president Henry Sidgwick, shortly
to become Professor of Moral Philosophy at Cambridge:
'From the recorded testimony of many competent witnesses
. . . there appears to be, amidst much illusion and deception,
an important body of remarkable phenomena, which are
primâ facie inexplicable on any generally recognised hypothesis, and which, if incontestably established, would be of
the highest possible value.'[23]

Such were the views of many highly respected late-nineteenth-century scholars and scientists who as declared spiritu-
alists, and in the face of considerable opposition, lent the
weight of their authority to the general revival of transcendentalism and occultism during the Age of Evolutionism.
Spiritualistic 'proofs' of mankind's survival of bodily death
promised to answer the desperate needs of educated men and
women who had lost their faith in Christianity. Such a man
was the poet and essayist F. W. H. Myers (1843-1901), a close
friend of Henry Sidgwick, and part-author of *Phantasms of
the Living* (1886). Meanwhile, at a semi-educated level,
*spiritual*ism was hailed as an omnicompetent refutation of
scientific *material*ism. Throughout the nineteenth century,
moreover, spiritualism retained its original connection with
Swedenborg's teachings, and numerous popular books on
spiritualism helped to keep alive and accessible, in its
Swedenborgian form, that doctrine of occult 'correspondences' between the everyday world and the spiritual world
which was to play so important a part in late-nineteenth-
century poetics.

An increasing awareness of traditional Indian religious
philosophies was probably the single most important factor
in the revival of transcendentalism in England during the
late nineteenth century. The translation of Indian sacred
literature into English, begun in the late eighteenth century
by such pioneers as Sir William Jones, was continued during
the latter half of the nineteenth century mainly by Friedrich
Max Müller, Professor of Comparative Philology at Oxford.

The importance of his work, in terms of the history of late-nineteenth-century ideas, has been admirably summarized by Alan Willard Brown as follows:

> Max Müller's monumental editing of translations of the great Eastern religious books revealed to sceptic, scientist, and believer alike a vast wealth of sacred and moral wisdom previously little known in the West, at the very time when Christian thinkers were being forced to find new sanctions for their belief in the Christian revelation.[24]

Max Müller's extremely popular Hibbert lectures, 'The Origin and Growth of Religion as Illustrated by the Religions of India', delivered in 1878, coincided with a large-scale awakening of interest in Indian religion and philosophy. The Theosophical Society, which had as its main aim the propagation of the doctrines of 'Esoteric Buddhism', had been founded in New York by Madame Blavatsky, Colonel H. S. Olcott and William Q. Judge in 1875, and *Lucifer: A Theosophical Monthly* had begun publication in England in 1877. Madame Blavatsky's *Isis Unveiled* had been published in 1877, and in 1879 Sir Edwin Arnold published *The Light of Asia,* a versified account of the life and teachings of the Buddha which has since run through countless editions. *The Occult World* and *Esoteric Buddhism,* two best-sellers by the leading Theosophical writer A. P. Sinnett, appeared in 1881 and 1883 respectively.

By 1884 the interest in Indian theology had grown large enough for Mrs Allmash, in a satire entitled 'Fashionable Philosophy', to announce: '. . . I quite dote on those dear old Shastras and Vedas, and Puranas; they contain such a lot of beautiful things, you know'.[25] The satire is by Laurence Oliphant (1829-88), the novelist, war-correspondent and mystic, who is best known for his satirical novel *Piccadilly* (1865). These were the days, according to the journalist and publicist Edmund Garrett (1865-1907), when a group of enthusiastic Cambridge undergraduates 'lived "the higher

life" on a course of Turkish baths and a date diet; while
three unlucky youths at Trinity nearly poisoned themselves
with hasheesh in an attempt to project their astral bodies,
and were only recovered at midnight by a relentless tutor
armed with the college authority and a stomach-pump'.[26]

A. P. Sinnett's *The Occult World* deals mainly with the
'occult phenomena' which he witnessed at Madame Blavatsky's Indian headquarters, including the letters supposedly
written to him by one of the 'Mahatmas', the occult *illumi-
nati* of Tibet whose emissary Madame Blavatsky claimed to
be. A large number of English readers found these reports
entirely credible, and some even took literally 'The Sisters
of Tibet', a perfectly obvious satire on Sinnett's book which
was first published by Laurence Oliphant in 1884. In 1885
the credibility of the Theosophical Society was however
considerably diminished by the two-hundred-page report on
Madame Blavatsky made by the Society for Psychical Research, which summed her up as 'one of the most accom-
plished, ingenious, and interesting impostors in history'.[27]

Theosophical writers such as Madame Blavatsky, A. P.
Sinnett and Annie Besant continued to attract intelligent
readers, nevertheless, and for four main reasons. Firstly, they
presented the human situation as something complex, meaningful, and exciting. The Theosophists saw the world as a
place in which spiritual values were paramount and free
will an actuality, and such views were in the strongest possible contrast to those based upon the gloomy tenets of High
Victorian materialistic determinism. *Isis Unveiled* and *The
Secret Doctrine* (1888) of Madame Blavatsky were published
at a time when Havelock Ellis and many similar young men
were searching for a more exalted view of human destiny
than the variety provided by such widely read writers as
David Strauss, Herbert Spencer, or the German materialist
philosopher Ernst Heinrich Haeckel (1834-1919). 'Orage,
like many others of his generation', writes his biographer
Philip Mairet, 'was fascinated by the "Secret Doctrine"—that

cosmic chaos of colossal symbols lit by auroral glimmerings
of magic.'[28]

Secondly, at a time when studies in comparative religion
were casting doubts on the validity of *individual* religions,
Theosophical writers presented Esoteric Buddhism as a
universal religion. According to A. P. Sinnett, Esoteric
Buddhism is the prototype or matrix of all subsequent religious belief: 'It is to spiritual philosophy much what Sanscrit
was found to be to comparative philology; it is a common
stock of philosophical roots. Judaism, Christianity, Buddhism
and the Egyptian theology are thus brought into one family
of ideas.'[29]

Thirdly, the Theosophists claimed that the doctrines of
Esoteric Buddhism were entirely consistent with recent scientific discoveries in the fields of geology, astronomy and
biology. The vast distances and periods of time postulated
in its cosmology corresponded perfectly with the discon-
certingly enlarged notions of the age of the earth and the
size of the universe which had been produced by recent
developments in geology and astronomy. Esoteric Buddhism,
says Sinnett, 'constitutes the only religious system that blends
itself easily with the physical truths discovered by modern
research in those branches of science. It not only blends itself
with . . . the nebula [*sic*] hypothesis and the stratification of
rocks, it rushes into the arms of these facts, so to speak, and
could not get on without them.'[30]

Fourthly, and most importantly, Esoteric Buddhism en-
visages all created things as gradually evolving over vast
periods of time to a condition of pure spirituality. It is in
short a system of religious belief which was exactly in accord
with those doctrines of evolutionary science which during the
late nineteenth century were sweeping all before them. As
Sinnett puts it:

> Esoteric science, though the most spiritual system im-
> aginable, exhibits, as running throughout Nature, the
> most exhaustive system of evolution that the human mind

can conceive. The Darwinian theory of evolution is simply an independent discovery of a portion—unhappily but a small portion—of the vast natural truth.[31]

It is noteworthy that Sinnett refers to Esoteric Buddhism as 'Esoteric *science*' (cf. Christian *Science,* another development of the period). The great attractiveness of Theosophical 'science' clearly lay in its claim to reconcile religious belief with crucial developments in the physical sciences, and with an increasing awareness of the non-Christian religions. In its attempt to reconcile the most ancient religion with the most modern science, it provides a particularly cogent example of the way in which generalized notions of evolution, extremely modern in their day, were used during the late nineteenth century as a new framework for old beliefs.

Madame Blavatsky's 'Mahatmas' were readily accepted as fact during the early 1880s probably because they had already been well known to readers of fiction for forty years. Bulwer Lytton's novel *Zanoni* (1842) largely concerns the exploits of two occult adepts named Zanoni and Mejnour, supposedly the sole surviving members of the original Rosicrucians. Their impressive supernatural powers include 'psychic telegraphy', while their possession of the *elixir vitae* has enabled them to live for many centuries. They are almost certainly the prototypes of Madame Blavatsky's own fictional creations.[32]

Zanoni and Lytton's other occult novel *A Strange Story* (1861-62) might both be described as 'sensation novels'. However, they are also philosophical fables which criticize the materialistic tradition of the French *Encyclopédistes* and affirm the values of philosophical idealism. In *A Strange Story,* for example, the creed of the hero, the young doctor Allen Fenwick, is at first that of 'a stern materialism'. On the last page of the novel, converted by the strange experiences which he has undergone, he affirms his new-found belief in the spiritual nature of the universe in the cry 'Above as below . . .!' This is a version of a famous hermetic dictum later to be quoted by W. B. Yeats in his poem 'Ribh Denounces Patrick' and by Arthur Symons in *The Symbolist Movement in Literature*: 'whatsoever is below, is like that which is above; and that which is above, is like that which is below'. Taken from the *Smaragdine Table* or *Emerald Tablet* traditionally ascribed to the Egyptian Neo-Platonic philosopher Hermes Trismegistus, this is another way of saying, with Plato, that the temporal world is a counterpart of the divine world.

Both *Zanoni* and *A Strange Story* make frequent mention of such topics as alchemy, 'magnetism', occultism, *maya*, astrology and mesmerism, such 'occult philosophers' as Plotinus, Paracelsus, Swedenborg, and even Eliphas Lévi, whose books so profoundly influenced the course of late-nineteenth-century French poetry. *Zanoni* also affirms the values of 'abstract' idealistic art against those of imitative realism. As Lytton was one of the most popular nineteenth-century novelists, there seems little doubt that these two novels were the single most effective means by which occult doctrines reached the general public. *A Strange Story*, which is both a popular compendium of occult doctrines and extremely forceful propaganda for them, was widely circulated in serial form in Dickens's *All the Year Round* during 1861, while *Zanoni* must surely rank as one of the most influential books of the second half of the nineteenth century. In the words of C. Nelson Stewart:

> If one were asked to name the book which more than any other provided a matrix for the building-up of modern theosophical philosophy in the English language, *Zanoni* seems the inevitable choice. Indeed, not only does a glance through the earlier literature published by the Theosophical Society never fail to reveal it as an oft-quoted book, but the advertisement pages show it being sold and translated as a kind of text-book.[33]

The well-known nineties poet Richard Le Gallienne first became aware of occultism through reading *Zanoni*,[34] and when Yeats in the introduction to his famous essay on magic describes an acquaintance who was inspired by reading one of Lytton's novels to devote 'much of his time and all his thought to magic',[35] we can hardly doubt that *Zanoni* was the novel in question.

Lytton's occult novels also paved the way for two other important developments of the period under discussion: the theory of symbolism and the doctrine of the evolutionary superman. The teachings of the French symbolists can hardly have surprised a generation of English poets already taught by Lytton that the only universal language is 'the language of symbol, in which all races [of spirits] that think—around, and above, and below us—can establish communion of thought',[36] whilst it is clear from Orage's writing that the Nietzschean gospel of the superman came to him not as a revolutionary concept but as confirmation of what Lytton had already written about Zanoni and Mejnour. Both *Zanoni* and *A Strange Story* were translated into French, and E. Drougard has argued for the direct influence of Lytton upon the work of Villiers de l'Isle-Adam.[37] If we accept Lytton as a profound influence on both the author of *Axël* and the foundress of the Theosophical Society, it follows that we must concede him a place of high importance in the development of late-nineteenth-century occultism and symbolism.

No survey of the main elements in the late-nineteenth-century revival of transcendentalism in England would be complete without some mention of the influence of Schopenhauer, whose idealist aesthetic appears to have been as influential in England as in France. In France, as A. G. Lehmann has shown, Schopenhauer's aesthetic was an extremely important source of symbolist theory.[38] In England it presumably underlies Walter Pater's famous and influential contention, in his essay 'The School of Giorgione' (1877), that 'All art constantly aspires towards the condition of music.'

Schopenhauer's philosophy and aesthetic had in fact been enthusiastically publicized in England by the music critic Francis Hueffer since the early 1870s. Hueffer was a German *emigré* who became a close friend of the Pre-Raphaelites, marrying Catherine, the daughter of the painter Ford Madox Brown, in 1872. The novelist Ford Madox Hueffer, who later called himself Ford Madox Ford, was their son.

Francis Hueffer, who had been a pupil of Schopenhauer, published his *Richard Wagner and the Music of the Future* in 1874. In this book he inaugurated a tendency in English criticism identical to that which took place in France during the late nineteenth century. In both countries, that is, the idealist aesthetic of Schopenhauer was given wide publicity by enthusiasts for the music of Wagner, whose own theoretical writings, such as the well-known essay on Beethoven of 1870, are often avowedly based upon Schopenhauer's philosophy of art. Wagner's own complete prose works were translated into English by William Ashton Ellis between 1892 and 1899. By this time R. B. Haldane and J. Kemp had published their English translation of Schopenhauer's *Die Welt als Wille und Vorstellung* (in 1883), and William Wallace, who had succeeded T. H. Green at Oxford, had published his extremely sympathetic *Life of Arthur Schopenhauer* (1890).

According to Schopenhauer, ultimate transcendent reality manifests itself in its purest and most direct form as Platonic ideas or archetypes, and in a less pure form at a further remove as earthly phenomena. All the arts have as their purpose the expression of these transcendental ideas, but music alone can express these directly, for it is the only art which is entirely non-representational. The other arts such as sculpture, painting and poetry can express the archetypal ideas but imperfectly. This is because they are necessarily restricted to the representation of earthly phenomena, and can therefore express the archetypes only at second hand, as it were. As Hueffer put it in 1874:

It is the aim of all the arts to express the eternal essence of things by means of these Platonic ideas, only music takes in this respect an exceptional position. Arts like painting and sculpture embody these ideas, as conceived by the artist through the medium of phenomena, the ideal value of which he shows, but only by the reproduction of their actual appearance. Even in poetry the realities of life and the visible wonders of the world, with their symbolic meaning, form an essential ingredient. . . . Music is not the copy of the ideas, like the other arts, but a representation of the cosmical will co-ordinate with the ideas themselves.[39]

Schopenhauer's philosophy being of so Buddhist a cast, it is not surprising that it proved congenial to the Theosophically minded; Wagner's English translator William Ashton Ellis, for example, was a prominent London Theosophist. Such was the prevailing spirit of evolutionary optimism among many of Schopenhauer's English commentators, however, that his fundamental pessimism appears to have been often ignored altogether. The following quotation from the poet Edward Carpenter, which for several important reasons makes an appropriate conclusion to our survey of the late-nineteenth-century revival of mysticism, mentions Schopenhauer in a characteristically cheerful way:

We seem to be arriving at a time when, with our circling of our knowledge of the globe, a great synthesis of all human thought on the ancient and ever-engrossing problem of Creation is quite naturally and inevitably taking shape. The world-old wisdom of the Upanishads, with their profound and impregnable doctrine of the universal Self, the teachings of Buddha or of Lao-Tzu, the poetic insight of Plato, the inspired sayings of Jesus and Paul, the speculations of Plotinus or of the Gnostics, and the wonderful contributions of later European thought from the fourteenth-century mystics down through Spinoza, Berkeley, Kant, Hegel, Schopenhauer, Ferrier and others;

all these, combining with the immense mass of material furnished by modern physical and biological Science and Psychology, are preparing a great birth, as it were; and out of this meeting of elements is already arising the dim outline of a philosophy which must surely dominate human thought for a long period.[40]

In its evolutionary optimism, extreme eclecticism, strong emphasis on transcendentalism and mysticism, and equally strong expectations of a *rapprochement* between modern science and religion, this passage could hardly be improved upon as an epitome of the major re-orientation of ideas whose most important aspects I have summarized above.

iii

Evolutionism greatly encouraged the revival of transcendentalism and occultism described above, which in its turn had important consequences for literary theory and aesthetics during the period 1880-1920. Evolutionism also greatly encouraged a revival of élitist views about society, and this in its turn had important consequences for critical thinking about literature, society, and the relationships between the two.

After 1880 it was increasingly argued that evolutionary progress could be maintained only by the creation of a new evolutionary aristocracy, that egalitarian societies based upon nineteenth-century ideals of Liberal democracy were consequently 'decadent', and that a new, authoritarian and hierarchical social structure was urgently necessary. Literary decadence was seen by some critics as the counterpart of social decadence, and calls for a return to social and literary 'order' were frequent. Ideas, analogies and assumptions of this kind run like a thread through the work of such otherwise disparate writers as T. E. Hulme, H. G. Wells, Alfred Orage, Cecil Chesterton, J. M. Kennedy and Wyndham Lewis, eventually culminating in the famous remark made by T. S. Eliot, in the preface to *For Lancelot Andrewes:*

Essays in Style and Order (1928) that his general point of
view might be described as 'classicist in literature, royalist in
politics, and anglo-catholic in religion'. In the final section
of this introductory chapter I show how evolutionistic thinking encouraged various literary critics of the period 1880-
1920 to believe in the desirability of an élite social class, and
how it also encouraged attacks upon the alleged decadence
of modern culture and the alleged degeneracy of modern
authors.

It is a characteristic paradox of the period 1880-1920 that
evolutionism should have led to a simultaneous exaltation
of the totalitarian corporate state on the one hand, and of
untrammelled individualism on the other. General ideas of
an all-controlling evolutionary force appear to have greatly
encouraged the view that the will of the individual citizen
should be subordinated to that of the State. 'The State', declared the English Hegelian philosopher Bernard Bosanquet
in 1899, 'is the fly-wheel of our life.'[41] In 1902, welcoming
the emergence of a new, authoritarian and hierarchical pattern of society, H. G. Wells suggested that this was 'the
expression of a greater Will'.[42] Over the space of thirty years,
on the other hand, Herbert Spencer's individualistic Law of
Evolution ('the transformation of the homogeneous into the
heterogeneous') had acquired something of the status of
divine revelation. *'Evolution is the law of life'*, asserts Oscar
Wilde unhesitatingly in 'The Soul of Man under Socialism',
'and there is no evolution except towards individualism.'[43]

These apparently contradictory notions were importantly
combined in the recommendation by Francis Galton, the
cousin of Charles Darwin, that the community as a whole
should deliberately set out to breed a 'highly gifted race
of men' or evolutionary aristocracy of superior individuals.
Galton first made this proposal as early as 1869, in the first
edition of his *Hereditary Genius*. He did not give the name
'eugenics' to his new 'science' until 1883, however, when he
described it as concerned with the breeding of human beings
who were 'hereditarily endowed with noble qualities'.[44] Now

that men's eyes had been opened to their high evolutionary destiny, he argued, it had become their 'religious duty'[45] to further the great work of evolution by fostering 'superior strains' of men and women and by discouraging the reproduction of 'sickly breeds'.

The increasing popularity of Galton's recommendations during the 1880s and 1890s led to the formation of a Eugenics Education Society in England in 1908 and the foundation of *The Eugenics Review* in 1909. Meanwhile, with the translation of *Also sprach Zarathustra* into English in 1896, the mythopoeic power of Nietzsche had strongly re-inforced Galton's 'scientific' advocacy of the superman. As will shortly be seen, however, evolutionary eagerness to produce a new race of geniuses was shot through with a profound anxiety born of the fear that men of genius as a class were innately mad, or degenerate, or both.

Elitist notions of the kind encouraged by the eugenicists are clearly reflected in the thought of Ellis and Orage, both of whom looked forward to a socialistic corporate state led by a new and 'highly gifted race of men'. Orage's guild socialism was a programme for a hierarchically structured commonwealth led by an evolutionary aristocracy, while for Ellis, writing in *The Task of Social Hygiene* in 1913, the breeding of a new élite is synonymous with the creation of socialism:

> the question of breed, the production of fine individuals, the elevation of the ideal of quality in human production over that of mere quantity, begins to be seen, not merely as a noble ideal in itself, but as the only method by which Socialism can be enabled to continue on its present path.[46]

Characteristically, though, the new 'science' of eugenics was used in support of political proposals which were very far from new. The 'Modern Utopia' announced by H. G. Wells in 1905 is no more than an evolutionistic refurbishing of Plato's two-thousand-year-old dream of an ideally integrated republic governed by an aristocratic caste of guardians. Orage's guild socialism, despite its evolutionist and Nietzschean trappings, is basically a programme for neo-feudalism, with its roots in that pervasive Victorian nostalgia for an idealized mediaeval society which dates at least as far back as Cobbett's *History of the Protestant Reformation* (1824), and which has been so well described in Alice Chandler's work *A Dream of Order: The Medieval Ideal in Nineteenth-Century English Literature* (1970).

Orage was in fact heavily indebted to the neo-feudalism which Disraeli had propounded some sixty years earlier under the name of 'Tory democracy'. For this reason certain aspects of his guild socialism met with the approval of various Tory men-of-letters, of whom T. E. Hulme is the best known. Two other such figures were Cecil Chesterton, the younger brother of G. K. Chesterton, and J. M. Kennedy. Cecil Chesterton was author of the Tory-democratic *Gladstonian Ghosts* (1906), and editor of *The Eye-Witness* (later *The New Witness*) between 1912 and 1916. J. M. Kennedy, the author of *Tory Democracy* (1911), was a regular contributor to *The New Age,* writing mainly on foreign affairs. He also translated several volumes of the standard English edition of Nietzsche's works edited by Dr Oscar Levy.

Sharing Orage's detestation of the Liberal middle classes and their *laissez-faire* creed of economic individualism, these Tory neo-feudalists welcomed his proposals for a unified hierarchical commonwealth of aristocrats and workers in which Liberals and their socially disruptive commercialism would have no place. 'We Tories', wrote J. M. Kennedy in *The New Age* of 1910, 'feel that we have much more in common with the Socialists than with the Liberals.'[47] In his *Tory Democracy* of the following year he welcomed Nietzsche as the latest exponent of the Tory-democratic tradition, and predicted that the working classes were rightly about to demand that a 'modified feudalism' replace the 'illusory freedom of the present heartless commercialism'.[48] The true social reformer, according to Kennedy, 'insists upon a well-

defined hierarchy and implicit obedience to leaders', and if
the philosophy of economic individualism were replaced by
the philosophy of 'leadership and subordination',[49] one consequence of the new hierarchical system would be the re-
organization of trades and crafts into the old form of guilds.

In judging the élitism of such 'men of 1914', which is reflected in the writings of Yeats and has proved repugnant to
so many of his readers, we should remember that the early-
twentieth-century élitists, unlike their influential predecessors such as Carlyle and Ruskin, believed their social policies
to be in accordance with scientifically valid 'laws of evolution'. Egalitarianism, in the Age of Evolutionism, was un-
scientific, and the ominous consequences of this type of
thinking are nowhere more apparent than in the obscene
last chapter of H. G. Well's *Anticipations* (1902). Published
less than twenty years after Galton had put the word
'eugenics' into circulation, this book cheerfully recommends
'good scientifically caused' torture as a punishment for crime,
the 'merciful obliteration' of the unfit, and the total ex-
tinction of the world's 'inferior [i.e. non-white] races'. Even
Arthur Symons, who expressed no interest whatsoever in
politics, reflects the élitism of his times. Throughout his
career he was at pains to present literature and the arts as
the province of an élite, and after the turn of the century
his attitudes towards 'the mob' became unmistakably more
violent.

It is of course heavily ironic, it should be noted in this
connection, that in his famous lecture 'The Two Cultures'
Sir Charles Snow should have held up his scientific hands
in pious horror at the wickedly reactionary political opinions
of Yeats, Pound and Wyndham Lewis, whose influence was
allegedly to ' "bring Auschwitz that much nearer" '.[50] The
readership and influence of these men-of-letters were as
nothing compared with those of the enormously influential
generation of enthusiastic eugenic scientists who preceded
them, and whose very existence Sir Charles conveniently
ignores. It was the élitism of scientists such as Galton which

helped make Auschwitz inevitable, while their particular brand of evolutionism greatly encouraged the militarism and chauvinism which twice devastated Western Europe in the first half of the twentieth century.

From about 1893, as Arthur J. Marder has pointed out, the English had regarded war as 'fairly imminent, inevitable, and not undesirable'.[51] Writing on British naval policy between 1880 and 1905, Marder demonstrates that this state of mind owed much to the spread of Darwinian notions. 'The British neo-Darwinians', he says, 'wrote that war was not simply a passing affliction, but a glorious and inevitable mode of progress, sanctioned by a law of nature. Every nation had become great through war, and the nation which did not and could not make war would deteriorate and cease to exist as a nation.' Furthermore, writes Marder:

> It was also held that the banners of civilization closely followed the march of the standards of war. The progress of humanity required the maintenance of the race struggle, physical, industrial, political, in which the weakest powers would go under, while the strongest and fittest would survive and flourish, because it was desirable that the world should be peopled, governed, and developed, as far as possible, by the races which could do the work best. This was how the world had progressed in the past, and how it must progress in the future.[52]

The prevalence of such notions should be borne in mind as we go on to examine the ideological background to the hysterical attacks which were mounted in England between 1890 and 1914 on literary 'decadence' and 'degeneration'.

During the last twenty years of the nineteenth century, evolutionist notions of decadence began to permeate three main branches of literary criticism: the historical, the cultural, and the biographical. The history of literary movements, according to John Addington Symonds's *Shakspere's Predecessors in the English Drama* (1884), follows an evolutionary pattern of 'preparation', 'maturity', and 'inevitable decadence'. Although this historical formula has lasted longest (being still in use today, though for the most part unconsciously), it did not have in its own day the immediate impact of the two formulae to be discussed here: the cultural formula which related the decadence of a literary work to the decadence of the society in which it is produced, and the biographical formula which related the decadence of a literary work to the biological degeneration of its author. Appearing at a time when it was becoming a religious duty to destroy whatever threatened to impede mankind's evolutionary progress, these two sets of pseudo-scientific notions greatly exacerbated public alarm about the dangers of decadent literature and degenerate authors.

As far as I have been able to discover it was the French poet, novelist and critic Paul Bourget (1852-1935) who first equated decadence in literature with decadence in social structure. He was certainly not the last. He first stated his influential 'théorie de la décadence' in a central passage of his essay on Baudelaire (1881), which was subsequently included in his *Essais de Psychologie Contemporaine* (1885). Havelock Ellis, who translated this passage in full in his 'A Note on Paul Bourget' of 1889, appears to have been responsible for introducing this 'theory' into England, as he was for introducing the equally influential ideas of the Italian criminologist Lombroso.

Entirely disregarding the *content* of literature, Bourget equates the decadence of a period's literary *style* with the decadence of the society from which it comes. In constructing this equation he relies upon the simple expedient of likening both language and society to organisms. The social organism functions correctly, according to Bourget, when the individual citizens of which it is composed behave in a correctly subordinate manner. Excessive individualism leads to social anarchy or decadence: 'The social organism . . . enters into decadence as soon as the individual life becomes exaggerated beneath the influence of acquired well-being, and of heredity.' When this type of insubordination occurs in language, the result is what Bourget calls a decadent style:

> A similar law governs the development and decadence of that other organism which we call language. A style of decadence is one in which the unity of the book is decomposed to give place to the independence of the page, in which the page is decomposed to give place to the independence of the phrase, and the phrase to give place to the independence of the word.[53]

Bourget's ludicrous equation of literary decadence with political individualism was given much wider currency in England after 1896, when Nietzsche's *Der Fall Wagner* was translated into English. In one of his earliest works Nietzsche had described culture as being above all 'the unity of artistic style, in every expression of the life of a people'.[54] In *The Wagner Case,* which is a late work, he borrowed Bourget's equation in order to attack the individualism and egalitarianism which he held responsible for the disunity and decadence of modern culture:

> I confine myself this time solely to the question of style. —What is the characteristic of all *literary décadence*? It is that the life no longer resides in the whole. The word gets the upper hand and jumps out of the sentence, the sentence stretches too far and obscures the meaning of the page, the page acquires life at the expense of the whole—the whole is no longer a whole. But that is the simile for every type of *décadence*: always anarchy of the atoms, disgregation of the will, in the language of morality, 'liberty of the individual,'—widened to a political theory, 'equal rights for all.'[55]

Bourget's equation is active and present, though not always explicitly, in the writings of several of *The New Age*'s leading contributors. 'It will be found . . . that every part of *The New Age* hangs together', wrote Orage in 1913 in connection with the overall policy of his magazine. '. . . The literature we despise', he says, 'is associated with the economics which we hate' (i.e. Liberal economic individualism), just as 'the literature we love is associated with the form of society we would assist in creating'.[56] Orage's own literary and artistic judgements were often based upon Bourget's formula, as will be seen in the chapter devoted to his criticism. 'Decadence', he writes typically, 'I have often defined as the substitution of the part for the whole; and in this sense Futurism is decadence in extremis.'[57]

In pre-1914 England the type of equation put forward by Bourget and Nietzsche greatly facilitated the task of dualistic cultural critics such as T. E. Hulme and J. M. Kennedy who opposed Conservatism to Liberalism, and classicism to romanticism. It enabled such critics to equate the politics they admired with the literature they admired, and the politics they despised with the literature they despised. Conservatism (i.e. neo-feudalism) could be implicitly equated with classicism on the following grounds: that the subordination of the citizens to the State in a hierarchical society corresponded to the subordination of the parts to the whole in a classical work of literature. Liberalism could be implicitly equated with romanticism on the converse grounds: that the social anarchy of individual economic competition corresponded to the stylistic anarchy of a romantic work of literature.

In his introduction to the *Further Speculations* of T. E. Hulme, Sam Hynes suggests that Hulme was the first English writer vigorously to assert a 'countercurrent' of views opposed to those of nineteenth-century Liberalism and romanticism:

> For this countercurrent in England Hulme is almost entirely responsible. He did not invent it, certainly— the charge that Hulme lacks originality is accurate, though irrelevant—but he was the first to assert it vigorously in England, and he provided the intellectual foundations, and prepared the audience, for the 'reactors' who followed him.[58]

Views resembling Hulme's are by no means uncommon in
The New Age after about 1909, however, and J. M. Kennedy
appears to be a key figure in this connection as in several
others. In a review in *The New Age* of 1909 he talks in terms
of a 'law' according to which degeneration occurs in both
literature and society:

> a period of strength, expansion, and conquest in a nation
> is, generally speaking, followed by a period of weakness,
> shrinkage, and degeneration. This law holds good in the
> realms of literature—the strong, expansive, healthy period
> of classicism is followed by a flaccid, shrinking, degen-
> erative period of romanticism.[59]

In the preface to his *Tory Democracy* (1911), which appeared in *The New Age* in serial form during its year of
publication, Kennedy equates Liberalism with romanticism,
and Conservatism with classicism. In his *English Literature
1880-1905*, which was published in 1912, he states that the
spread of the 'slow poison of Romanticism' in England
during the nineteenth century was aided by the ' "Liberal"
trend of thought' which is its usual accompaniment.[60]

It comes as no great surprise to find Kennedy praising
Matthew Arnold as 'our one really great critic of the nineteenth century',[61] for what I have called Bourget's formula
does little more than express in biological language and
dogmatically simplified form some of the distinctions already
made by Arnold in 1869 between 'culture' on the one hand
and 'anarchy' on the other. We are reminded once again
that the Age of Evolutionism was one in which established
notions were being reformulated and recirculated in new
and pseudo-scientific trappings. The very notion of society
as an 'organism' upon which Bourget and his successors de-
pend is likewise a thoroughly traditional one. Herbert Spencer had in fact already found new sanctions for this notion,
characteristically based upon the latest discoveries of 'biological science', in an important early essay of 1860.[62]

Of the many other traditional notions which acquired the new and often dangerous sanction of alleged scientific proof during the Age of Evolutionism, a belief in the degeneracy of the current human species was perhaps the most commonplace. Another such traditional belief, as we shall see, was that 'Great wits are sure to madness near allied', a notion profoundly disquieting to the advocates of a new breed of evolutionary geniuses.

Degeneration by Professor E. Ray Lankester, the first evolutionist work to be published on this topic in England, appeared on the scene with uncanny promptitude in 1880. It is generally assumed, says Lankester, who was Professor of Zoology at University College, London, from 1874 until 1891, that the white races of Europe are making evolutionary progress. They may in fact be *degenerating,* and the imminent collapse of Western civilization can be avoided only by discovering from the general laws of evolution whatever assists the progress of the race. The scientific evidence for Lankester's grandiose and alarming hypothesis, which he himself admits to be extremely tentative, rests upon certain characteristics of 'our ruined cousins—the degenerate Ascidians'.[63] The Ascidians are not a once-great race of human beings, alas, but a variety of sea-squirt.

As we have seen in our earlier comments on the élitism of the period, Galton introduced the term 'eugenics' in 1883. Between that date and 1914 public discussion of alleged racial, physical, moral, sexual and literary degeneration reached obsessive proportions in England, and remedies were frequently sought in proposals for 'eugenic reform'. Discussion of these issues was particularly rife after the founding of the Eugenics Education Society in 1908. *The New Age,* for example, contains numerous articles on eugenics between 1908 and 1914, and during these years Havelock Ellis published *The Problem of Race-Regeneration* (1911) and *The Task of Social Hygiene* (1913), two works noticeably lacking in the violence and the dogmatism of most eugenic writing of the period. Although *The Problem of Race-Regeneration* is one of a number of 'New Tracts for the Times', it is in fact quite opposed to the assumptions about degeneration and the alarmist tone of the general editor of this series, whose language may be taken as typical. The authors of these tracts consider, in the words of this gentleman, such grave and urgent questions as 'the uncontrolled multiplication of the degenerate, who threaten to swamp in a few generations the purer elements of our race'.[64] The tracts were published by the National Council of Public Morals under the presidency of the Lord Bishop of Durham.

The suggestion that artists and men-of-letters are by nature 'degenerates' appears to have been first made by the Italian pioneer of criminal anthropology Cesare Lombroso (1836-1909) in *L'Uomo di Genio* (1888). In this book, which was translated into English by Havelock Ellis in 1891, Lombroso claimed that 'the signs of degeneration are found more frequently in men of genius than even in the insane'.[65] In 1891 there also appeared a work by the well-known journalist J. F. Nisbet (1851-99), who was dramatic critic for *The Times* from 1882 onwards. In this book, which is entitled *The Insanity of Genius,* Nisbet, using literary men among his examples, claimed to 'place upon a solid basis of fact the long-suspected relationship of genius and insanity'.[66] In the second edition of *Hereditary Genius,* which appeared in the following year, and which contains chapters on literary men, poets, painters and musicians, Francis Galton agreed with Lombroso that there was 'a painfully close relation'[67] between insanity and genius. By this time Havelock Ellis (in *The Criminal,* 1890) had described the vanity of literary men as a sign of their 'tendency . . . to degeneration',[68] and had discussed the Decadent poet Verlaine as 'an interesting example of the man of genius who is also distinctly a criminal'.[69]

In *The Man of Genius* Lombroso specifically equates literary decadence with biological degeneration in a section of his chapter, 'Literary and Artistic Mattoids'. In this section, which is devoted to the French Decadents, he concludes from the evidence of a piece of vulgar journalism that 'the *décadents* correspond exactly to the diagnosis of literary mattoids, in all their old vacuity, but with the appearance of novelty'.[70]

In his 'Conclusions' Lombroso expresses the hope that his book may 'afford an experimental starting-point for a criticism of artistic and literary . . . creations'.[71] This hope was soon fulfilled in the *Entartung* (1892-93) of Max Nordau (1849-1923), the German-Hungarian physician and author. Dedicated to Lombroso, *Entartung* (*Degeneration*) investigates current fashions in art and literature in order to prove that 'they have their source in the degeneracy of their authors, and that the enthusiasm of their admirers is for manifestations of more or less pronounced moral insanity, imbecility, and dementia'.[72] With a wealth of documentation Nordau proceeds to demonstrate in an alarming and apparently scientific way that the leading literary figures of the day are without exception 'degenerates' and 'mattoids'. His demonstrations in fact rest upon nothing more substantial than spurious covert syllogisms of the following type: the language of the insane is disjointed; the language of Verlaine's poems is disjointed; Verlaine is consequently insane.

Degeneration was the Age of Evolutionism's most influential work of literary criticism. The first edition of the English translation, which appeared in February 1895, was followed by no less than seven further impressions during the same year. The book's enormous popularity in England appears to have been a direct result of the trial of Oscar Wilde, with which publication of the English translation may well have been designed to coincide. Several pages of Nordau's work are in fact devoted to Wilde, and notions of homosexual 'degeneracy' doubtless reinforced in the popular mind the important link already made by Lombroso and Nordau between biological degeneration on the one hand and literary decadence on the other. Mr Punch complained in the spring of 1895 that 'Morbid sickliness surrounds us in our lives, our books, our art',[73] whilst a reviewer in *The Academy,* suddenly made aware by Nordau of the 'blackest horrors' of the 'Ibsenites and Tolstoi-ites and Pornographists and Dirt-Eaters' whom he had formerly admired, called for 'Glorious bonfires of bad books!'[74]

Among the more prominent mattoids and degenerates discussed by Nordau were Whitman, Zola, Ibsen, Nietzsche and Huysmans: precisely the authors recommended as moral teachers and men of religion by Havelock Ellis in *The New Spirit* and *Affirmations.* One of Nordau's comments on Nietzsche, to whom he devoted an entire chapter of *Degeneration,* will reveal something of the extremely hostile climate of opinion in which Ellis published his pioneering essays on Nietzsche in *The Savoy* during 1896. Nordau describes Nietzsche as:

> a madman, with flashing eyes, wild gestures, and foaming mouth, spouting forth deafening bombast; and through it all, now breaking out into frenzied laughter, now sputtering expressions of filthy abuse and invective, now skipping about in a giddily agile dance, and now bursting upon the auditors with threatening mien and clenched fists.[75]

During the Age of Evolutionism, as we have seen, many established ideas found new and pseudo-scientific sanctions. Evolutionism greatly encouraged the revival of religious mysticism described in the earlier part of this chapter. It also greatly encouraged savage attacks on new and experimental forms of art and literature on the grounds that they were detrimental to the evolutionary progress of the race, and the hysterical abusiveness of Nordau became increasingly typical of English cultural criticism as the period developed. It will already be apparent that Havelock Ellis played an important part in the introduction into England of continental notions of artistic decadence and degeneration. This and other aspects of Ellis's criticism are discussed in the chapter which follows.

2

The New Hellenism
Havelock Ellis

Henry Havelock Ellis was born on 2 February 1859 at Croydon in Surrey. Until the age of eleven he attended the French and German College at Merton, and until the age of sixteen he was a weekly boarder at a small private school at Mitcham.

His father was master of a sailing-ship, and at the age of seven Ellis sailed round the world with him, visiting Australia and South America. In 1875, at the age of sixteen, he set sail with his father to Calcutta, but for reasons of health disembarked in Sydney. He remained in New South Wales for four years, working as a school-teacher in the Australian bush. It was during these years that he underwent the religious conversion described earlier, as a result of reading James Hinton's *Life in Nature*. He also decided to study medicine as James Hinton had done, and in particular to devote his life to the study of human sexuality.

Ellis returned to England in 1879, having celebrated his twentieth birthday *en route* from Australia. He began his medical studies at St Thomas's Hospital a year later, eventually qualifying as a medical practitioner in 1889 but never setting up in independent practice. While studying medicine in London between 1880 and 1889 Ellis wrote a considerable number of articles on literature, philosophy and social questions, and also found time to be an active member of both the Progressive Association and the Fellowship of the New Life, that seminal group from which the Fabian Society was to spring. His first published article, on Rubens, appeared in *The Pen* in 1880. In 1884 he was invited to review books for *Mind,* and in 1886 he became reviewer of theological books for *The Westminster Review.*

In 1886 he also began the Mermaid series of editions of Elizabethan and Jacobean dramatists published by Henry Vizetelly, himself editing the volumes of works by Marlowe, Middleton and Ford. In 1888 he edited *The Pillars of Society, and Other Plays,* the first collection of Ibsen's plays to be published in England. Following Vizetelly's prosecution for publishing the work of Zola, which took place in 1889, Ellis lost his general editorship of the Mermaid series. He then became general editor of the Contemporary Science series for the firm of Walter Scott, and this series, which continued until 1914, provided him with a modest living for twenty-five years.

In 1884 Ellis had met the South African novelist Olive Schreiner, whose *The Story of an African Farm* had been published the year before. They appear to have become engaged, but did not marry. Olive Schreiner returned to South Africa in 1889, and in 1891 Ellis married Edith Lees, a fellow-member of the Fellowship of the New Life.

Ellis's search for other editors for the Mermaid series led to two important friendships, firstly with John Addington Symonds, with whom he later collaborated on the first edition of *Sexual Inversion,* and secondly with Arthur Symons, to whose work he had been attracted by an article on the French poet Mistral in *The National Review* of January 1886. Symons was to become his lifelong friend and travelling-companion, and in 1890 the two young men visited Paris together for three months, making the acquaintance of the leading Symbolist poets and painters.

It was in this year that Ellis published his first two books: a collection of literary essays entitled *The New Spirit,* and a work of criminal anthropology entitled *The Criminal.* The latter book was based upon the work of Lombroso, whose

The Man of Genius he translated and published in the following year.

In 1894 Ellis joined Symons at Fountain Court in the Temple, where he continued to occupy rooms in Symons's chambers until the latter's marriage in 1901. During 1896 Ellis contributed to most of the eight issues of Symons's short-lived periodical *The Savoy*, later publishing several of these essays in his volume of *Affirmations* (1898).

The first volume of Ellis's *Studies in the Psychology of Sex* was published in 1897. Concerned with sexual inversion, it had been begun in collaboration with John Addington Symonds, who had died in 1893. In 1898 one George Bedborough was prosecuted and fined for selling copies of this book in England, and subsequent volumes of *Studies in the Psychology of Sex* were therefore published in the United States. Having read the *Studien über Hysterie* of Freud and Breuer in 1896, Ellis was to become during the next twenty years one of the leading interpreters of psychoanalytic concepts to British readers. His own terms 'auto-erotism' and 'narcissism' became part of the established language of psychoanalysis.

In 1900, as a counter to current eulogies of the century just ended, Ellis published his satirical dialogue *The Nineteenth Century*, and during 1903 and 1904 he contributed several literary articles to *The Weekly Critical Review*, a bi-lingual periodical which was published in Paris. In 1904 he published two major works: *A Study of British Genius*, which takes as its starting-point Francis Galton's studies in hereditary genius, and *The World of Dreams*, his collected studies in the psychology of dreaming. His major synthetic work, *The Dance of Life*, was published in 1923, and *From Rousseau to Proust*, a collection of essays on French literature, in 1936.

Havelock Ellis died in 1939. His autobiography (*My Life*), which he had begun to write in 1899, was published posthumously in 1940.

ii

The climate of evolutionism, as shown in Chapter 1, was favourable to a revival of various forms of mysticism at a time when orthodox Christian beliefs were regarded by many as no longer tenable. Each of the three critics discussed in this book adopted and proclaimed some form of mystical doctrine: Symons a type of Neo-Platonism, Orage a type of Theosophy, and Ellis a type of biological vitalism. In the first section of the present chapter, I begin by tracing Ellis's views on the relationship of mysticism to science, and show that he was finally to invoke the prestige of science as a means of rehabilitating a world-view which was more mediaeval than modern. I then discuss the impact of evolutionary science upon his approach to literary criticism.

Throughout his career, Ellis, whose overt commitment to science sharply distinguishes his thinking from that of Orage and Symons, strongly advocated a *rapprochement* between science and mysticism. We have already seen that during his stay in Australia he was converted to a form of vitalistic mysticism on reading Hinton's *Life in Nature*. On his return to England at the beginning of the Age of Evolutionism we find him reading a considerable number of books connected with mysticism: Max Müller's *Lectures on the Vedas,* Ribot's *Schopenhauer et sa Philosophie,* Francis Hueffer's *Musical Studies,* Gilchrist's *The Life of William Blake,* and Overton's *Nonjuror and Mystic,* which is a biography of William Law, the eighteenth-century English disciple of the famous mystic Jacob Boehme.[1]

In 1884 he writes in much the same vein concerning religious controversy as Benjamin Kidd was to do in his *Social Evolution* of ten years later. He mocks as behind the times those who are still attacking 'the corpses and ghosts' of Christian dogma, and states that 'there are no longer any signs worth heeding . . . that the religious question is still attracting the energy which it formerly absorbed'.[2] He himself, reviewing theological books during 1886 for *The*

Westminster Review, displays a marked leaning towards
Taoist mysticism.

Reviewing Edward Carpenter's *Towards Democracy* in
the same year, he drew particular attention to 'the element
of mystic religion' in Carpenter's work, saying that:

> We are compelled to regard it—after the sexual passion
> which is the very life of the race itself—as man's strongest
> and most persistent instinct. So long as it is saved from
> fanaticism by a strenuous devotion to science, by a
> perpetual reference to the moral structure of society, it
> will always remain an integral portion of the whole man
> in his finest developments.[3]

Ellis's attempt to synthesize science and religious mysticism
is especially apparent in *The New Spirit* (1890), the title
of which is a direct expression of his own evolutionary
optimism. In the introduction to this book, for example, he
attributes the inauguration of a new era to the concept of
evolution, which 'has penetrated every department of organic
science, especially where it touches man'.[4] In the conclusion
to *The New Spirit* Ellis attempts to make clear to himself
the 'vast and many-shaped religious element of life'. Starting
out from the proposition that 'The old dispute between
mind and matter no longer has any significance', he proceeds to argue that whatever brings about a 'joyous expansion' of the soul, or its aspiration towards the infinite, is
religious. This joyous expansion may be brought about by
art, science, nature, or the exemplary lives of great men.
Above all it is the product of that mystical 'intuition of union
with the world' which is the message of the world's great
religions:

> The supreme expression of the religious consciousness
> lies always in an intuition of union with the world, under
> whatever abstract or concrete names the infinite not-self
> may be hidden. . . . It is this intuition which is the
> 'emptiness' of Lâo-Tze. . . . This is the great good news of

the Upanishads: the *âtman,* the soul, may attain to a state
of *yoga,* of union, with the supreme *âtman.* . . . This is
the great assertion of Christ, 'I and my Father are one'.
. . . And that again is but in another form the Sufiism
of Jelal-ed-din—the mystic union of the human bride-
groom with the Divine Bride.[5]

It is clear that Ellis's mysticism, like Carpenter's, was extremely eclectic, and that he writes as one who is, in his own
words, 'enfranchised from creeds'.

In *The New Spirit* Ellis also voices his concern lest religious experience paralyse men's 'motor energies of life', however, and as the revival of mysticism spread during the
1890s he found it necessary to disassociate himself from what
he regarded as other-worldly rejections of the life of nature
and reason. On every hand, he writes in 1898, we see 'occultism, theosophy, spiritualism, all those vague forms on the
borderland of the unknown which call to tired men weary
of too much living . . . to hide their faces from the sun of
nature'.[6] Holding it foolish to resent this tendency, though,
Ellis tolerantly adjures his contemporaries to steep themselves in such doctrines, in full confidence that they will
eventually return to the classic party of nature and rationalism.

Ellis did not return to the issue of science and mysticism
until 1913. By this time, what remained of the oppressive
world-view derived from High Victorian physics had been
finally put to flight by such mathematical physicists as Max
Planck, J. J. Thomson, Ernest Rutherford and Albert Einstein. This major shift in thought is reflected in Ellis's
writing. Until recently, he writes, the concept of matter has
been 'of primary importance . . . in creating an artificial
opposition between science and religion'. Now that matter
is coming to be regarded as 'merely an electrical emanation',
we are evidently approaching a time when 'The spontaneous
affirmation of the mystic that he lives in the spiritual world

here and now, will . . . be . . . merely the same affirmation which the man of science has more laboriously reached.'[7]

Under the title of 'The Art of Religion' this article of 1913, which had originally been entitled 'Science and Mysticism', was reprinted in Ellis's *The Dance of Life* (1923). In the preface to this major synthetic work he argues that the discoveries of the mathematical physicists of the early twentieth century herald a 'classico-mathematical Renaissance' comparable to that of seventeenth-century France:

> We, too, witness a classico-mathematical Renaissance. It is bringing us a new vision of the universe, but also a new vision of human life. That is why it is necessary to insist upon life as a dance. This is not a mere metaphor. The dance is the rule of number and of rhythm and of measure and of order, of the controlling influence of form, of the subordination of the parts to the whole. That is what a dance is. And these same properties also make up the classic spirit, not only in life, but, still more clearly and definitely, in the universe itself. We are strictly correct when we regard not only life but the universe as a dance. For the universe is made up of a certain number of elements, less than a hundred, and the 'periodic law' of these elements is metrical.[8]

Although Ellis in this preface employs such extremely up-to-date touchstones as Albert Einstein and the Russian Ballet, the new 'classico-mathematical' view of the world which he presents is of course thoroughly traditional. Ellis restates, in twentieth-century terms, that mediaeval view of the world as an orderly, unified and hierarchical cosmic dance which E. M. W. Tillyard has so well described in *The Elizabethan World-Picture*. In doing so he arrives, though by a dissimilar route, at a type of neo-feudalism which has many similarities to the guild socialism of Orage and his colleagues, who were also enthusiasts for 'order', 'the classic spirit', and 'the subordination of the parts to the whole'. Like so many of his less scientifically minded contemporaries, Ellis employed the latest scientific theories in support of thoroughly traditional notions about man, society, and the universe.

Havelock Ellis's mysticism, like that of Arthur Symons and Alfred Orage, was accompanied by a claim that the meaning of works of art and literature could not be rationally discussed or understood, but could be grasped only by 'imaginative insight'. This aspect of his criticism is interesting more from the theoretical point of view than the practical, however, and I therefore postpone discussion of it until my final chapter. In practice, Ellis's religious mysticism had far fewer consequences for his criticism than did his interest in evolutionary anthropology and psychology, which I now go on to discuss.

The rapidly growing prestige of science and the scientific method during the period 1880-1920 is occasionally reflected in the writings of both Symons and Orage. Of the three critics under particular discussion, however, only Ellis was strongly influenced by the scientific thought of the day. As early as 1885 he was calling for literary criticism to be placed upon a properly scientific footing, and referring to criticism itself as 'a complex development of psychological science'.[9] In his preface to *The New Spirit* he describes his intention as being to record 'as impersonally as may be' the spirit of the age as represented by certain literary personalities, and refers to his essays on these figures as so many 'sphygmographic tracings'.[10] Ellis's scientific interests frequently go hand in hand with interests of quite another kind, however, and he was later to acknowledge that *The New Spirit* was really 'a personal document put into an impersonal shape' through which he could present his own 'most intimate feelings'.[11] Much of his criticism is equally ambivalent. While discussing an author from the standpoint of one who is ostensibly conducting a scientific investigation into the psychology of genius in men-of-letters, Ellis may also be putting before the reader his own *avant-garde* views on sexual morality or literary censorship. These views themselves will be discussed in the second major section of this chapter. I confine myself for the moment to the influence of evolutionary science upon his approach to criticism.

In his rôle of scientific investigator Ellis concerns himself but little with the meaning of works of art and literature. His main interest here is in the personalities of artistic men of genius as revealed by their works. The work is 'explained' as the product of a particular temperament, and the temperament itself is then 'explained' as the product of particular geographical and ancestral influences. In *The New Spirit*, for example, Ellis claims that Ibsen's tendency 'to philosophic abstraction and . . . strenuous earnestness, mingling with the more characteristically northern imaginative influences, are explained by' his mixed Scottish and German ancestry.[12] On one occasion he even goes so far as to claim that the peculiarities of Addison's prose-style are the consequence of his Scandinavian heredity.[13] On another occasion, however, he is willing to concede that 'we can by no means altogether account for Huysmans by race and environment'.[14]

The words 'race' and 'environment' indicate the ultimate sources of Ellis's scientific criticism, as does his early patronizing remark that Landor as a critic 'belonged to a school that flourished before Sainte-Beuve and Taine had re-created criticism'.[15] The critical notions of *race* and *milieu* developed by Sainte-Beuve and Taine possessed little novelty at the time at which Ellis was writing. For the first time, however, they were being examined from a professionally scientific point of view, and this at a time when the sciences were becoming increasingly dominated by evolutionistic assumptions. Man himself, regarded as a creature still evolving, was becoming the object of would-be scientific study on the part of psychologists and anthropologists, and as Ellis himself points out in his introduction to *The New Spirit*, the year in which *On the Origin of Species* was published was also a year of crucial importance for the science of anthropology:

> Our hopes for the evolution of man, and our most indispensable guide, are bound up with all that we can

learn of man's past and all that we can measure of his present. It was by a significant coincidence that that great modern science which has man himself for its subject was created by Broca, when he founded the Société d'Anthropologie of Paris in the same memorable year of 1859 which first saw 'The Origin of Species.'[16]

In the same year, as he pointed out in his autobiography, 'Moreau de Tours initiated the psychological study of genius; and Lombroso conceived that idea of the anthropological method of studying criminals and other abnormal groups which in its transformations has proved so fruitful'.[17] Born in the same memorable year of 1859, Ellis was exactly of an age to be influenced by these new and exciting developments, and the writings of Galton (in particular) and Lombroso clearly led to what is his major interest as a scientific critic: the ancestry and psychology of men of genius.

Ellis appears to have begun as an enthusiastic disciple of Lombroso, but to have rejected Lombroso's association of genius with insanity in the years following the English publication of Nordau's *Degeneration*. We have already seen in Chapter 1 that he translated *The Man of Genius,* in which Lombroso associates genius with degeneration and insanity, at a time when he himself had already claimed Verlaine as 'an interesting example of the man of genius who is also distinctly a criminal'. In the second number of *The Savoy* he also translated an article by Lombroso entitled 'A Mad Saint', a clinical study in religious mania which leads to the conclusion that 'The germ of holiness, as well as that of genius, must be sought among the insane.'[18]

Writing after the turn of the century, however, Ellis was to state that 'the doctrine of the insanity of genius, notwithstanding many thorough-going champions, may be said to be finally discredited'.[19] Described by a Dr Mercier as a devoted follower of Lombroso, Ellis in 1919 replied in these words: 'Lombroso founded a vigorous school of investigators, but I have never formed part of it. I was merely an

outsider who enjoyed the spectacle.'[20] Coming from one who
had been instrumental in bringing Lombroso's views before
the British public in the early 1890s, and who had thus
helped pave the way for subsequent outcries against literary
degeneration and decadence, the statement seems disingenu-
ous in the extreme.

More durable than that of Lombroso, Galton's influence
upon Ellis is at its most evident in his article of 1893 entitled
'The Ancestry of Genius'. This is intended as a contribution
to what Ellis calls the 'etiology' of genius, and it is worth
remarking in passing that the word 'etiology' connotes not
merely causation but disease. In this article Ellis examines
'the ancestry of some of the chief English poets and imaginative writers of recent years, with reference to the question of
race'. He describes the ancestry of five poets of generally
acknowledged genius (Tennyson, Browning, Swinburne,
Rossetti and Morris) and of seven other living writers, who
include his friends Olive Schreiner and Roden Noel. The
proportion of 'mixed and foreign blood' in these two groups,
he finds, is much greater than Galton found in an average
group, and much greater than Galton found in his enquiries
into British geniuses in the scientific field:

> While we have found that among twelve eminent British
> imaginative writers no less than ten show more or less
> marked traces of foreign blood, and not one can be said
> to be pure English, Mr. Galton found that out of every
> ten distinguished British scientific men five were pure
> English, and only one had foreign blood.

Great poets and artists, he concludes, are the result of cross-
breeding between two European races of men, the tall and
fair Nordic race, and the short and dark Celtic race, and the
British Isles continue as ever to form 'a well-arranged pair
of compact electric batteries for explosive fusion of the
two elements'.[21]

The identical notion recurs thirteen years later in Ellis's
essay 'The Celtic Spirit in Literature', in which he claims

that 'until we realise clearly what the Celtic spirit means and what the Nordic spirit means we are without the clue to guide us through our literature'. This clue, he goes on to say, can be found only 'when we place ourselves at a standpoint at once psychological and ethnological. As we follow it, our rich and varied literature, for the first time, falls into harmonious order.'[22]

In his article of 1896, 'The Colour-Sense in Literature', Ellis seems at first to turn from extreme generalities of this biographical kind to the actual words of which works of literature are composed. In this article he provides statistical tables showing the frequency with which the names of basic colours appear in the works of a number of British poets from Chaucer onwards. This technique, he claims, 'enables us to take a definite step in the attainment of a scientific aesthetic, by furnishing a means of comparative study'. The subject of this comparative study is not however the meaning of the poems in which these colour-words appear, but the personalities of the poets themselves. His statistical tables, according to Ellis, are 'an instrument for investigating a writer's personal psychology, by defining the nature of his aesthetic colour-vision'.[23] Psychological investigations of this kind, it appears elsewhere, can be carried out quite independently of the history of art and literature. We may read Vasari as art-historians, says Ellis, introducing his edition of *Lives of the Italian Painters* in 1895, or 'for the light which he throws on the psychology of genius in artists. . . . It is solely from this point of view that the reader will approach Vasari in the present volume.'[24]

On two occasions in *Affirmations* Ellis introduces the more recent concept of psychological sublimation in order to 'explain' artistic creativity. In his essay on Casanova he states that 'A certain degree of continence—I do not mean merely in the region of sex but in the other fields of human action also—is needed as a breeding-ground for the dreams and images of desire to develop into the perfected visions of art.'[25] In his discussion of Zola he finds the basis of Zola's fictional methods in the deprivations which the novelist suffered as a child:

> During long years . . . Zola, as a child and youth, suffered from poverty, poverty almost amounting to actual starvation, the terrible poverty of respectability. The whole temper of his work and his outlook on the world are clearly conditioned by this prolonged starvation of adolescence. . . . Zola's literary methods are those of the *parvenu* who has tried to thrust himself in from outside, who has never been seated at the table of life, who has never really lived.[26]

At the time at which Ellis was writing, this was probably a novel contribution to the developing 'science' of psychoanalysis, which has itself been frequently employed since to prolong into the twentieth century the biographical literary criticism of the nineteenth. In investigating the psychology of artistic genius in his critical essays, however, Ellis relies almost entirely on the older notions of *race* and *milieu*, showing a marked preference for the former as modified by Galton's views on hereditary influences.

The Age of Evolutionism was fascinated by 'genius' and sought anxiously to discover how it arose, how it was transmitted, how its transmission could be controlled in the interests of evolutionary progress, and whether it was not in fact a treacherous aberration which would lead directly to the nightmare of evolutionary decline. In the type of scientific criticism to which he aspired, and in one of the major emphases of his own critical essays, Ellis was clearly indebted to speculations concerning hereditary genius which were current during the Age of Evolutionism. Despite their strongly biographical approach, however, his critical essays are also a platform for the presentation of his own radical views on society and literature, as he himself acknowledges in the preface to *Affirmations*. These views are described in the section immediately following, in which I discuss his three books *The New Spirit, Affirmations,* and *The Nineteenth Century,* together with his separate essays on Paul Bourget, Edward Carpenter, and Thomas Hardy.

iii

Sometimes openly and sometimes obliquely, Ellis uses his critical essays to support whatever in his view makes for individual unity of being, especially freedom of sexual expression. He also uses them to oppose whatever in his view prevents the achievement of this unity, especially Christianity, literary censorship, and commercialism. What he supports he generally calls classicism, and what he opposes he sometimes calls decadence. His use of these terms lacks the political connotations which they acquired at the hands of the *New Age* writers, however, except in the preface to *The Dance of Life,* where he appears to have incorporated some of their ideas.

Writing on Landor in the introduction to his 1886 edition of *Imaginary Conversations,* Ellis praises him because the classical qualities of 'clear outline and sane simplicity' in his prose outweigh the romantic qualities of 'picturesque profusion'.[27] He rarely employs the word 'classical' in a purely literary sense, however. Instead, he uses it much more broadly to denote a whole way of life. The immediate ancestor of Ellis's classicism is in fact the Hellenism of Swinburne, especially as expressed in Swinburne's 'The Last Oracle'. This poem tells us that the whole world has been made to 'moan with hymns of wrath and wrong' since the chant of well-adjusted Hellenes was supplanted by the wail of guilt-ridden Christians.

Swinburne however had not realized that the latest discoveries of modern science might be called in to rehabilitate his Hellenic ideals. It was consequently John Addington Symonds, who had learned this primary lesson of the Age of Evolutionism, whom Ellis in his essay 'The Present Position of English Criticism' (1885) singled out as representing

'whatever is best' in the criticism of the day. Symonds, says
Ellis:

> declares that there is but one way to make the Hellenic
> tradition vital—to be natural. Science, he adds, will place
> the future man on a higher pinnacle than even the
> Greek; for it has given us the final discovery that there
> is no antagonism, but rather a most intimate connection
> between the elements of our being. It is largely because
> Mr. Symonds is so resolute to live in this conception of
> the whole . . . that he represents to-day whatever is best
> in English criticism.[28]

In his review of Edward Carpenter's *Towards Democracy* in
the same year, Ellis makes clearer what he had intended by
the Hellenic 'conception of the whole' for which he had
praised John Addington Symonds:

> Like Walt Whitman, Mr. Carpenter has a profound sense
> of the mystery and significance of the body: he cannot
> see any salvation for man till he is able to enter into pure
> and frank relation with his own body, the latest and best
> gift of nature, so long concealed; it is by his body, he
> insists, that man ascends and knows himself and he can-
> not treat it too reverently. 'The body is the root of the
> soul.'[29]

A similar enthusiasm for authors who oppose a dualistic
concept of body and soul is apparent in the selection of
Heine's work which Ellis published in 1887. In his introduction to this selection Ellis praises the Hellenic ideals of
Heine. He also draws particular attention to Heine's essay
'Religion and Philosophy in Germany', in which Heine concludes his account of the Gnostic and Manichaean influences
upon Christianity with the following words:

> When once mankind shall have recovered its perfect life,
> when peace shall be again restored between body and
> soul, and they shall again interpenetrate each other with

their original harmony, then it will be scarcely possible to comprehend the factitious feud which Christianity has instigated between them.[30]

The introduction to Ellis's selection from Heine is one of the essays included in *The New Spirit* in 1890. Here it forms part of a schematic approach to literature and ideas which is clearly based upon that employed by Paul Bourget in his two volumes of *Essais de Psychologie Contemporaine*. Ellis had read these works avidly when they were published in 1885 and 1886, and like Bourget he treats each of his literary figures 'with reference to the current influence which it represents'[31] in the development of ideas.

Unlike Bourget, however, Ellis is highly optimistic about these developments. In his introduction he enthusiastically prophesies a major renascence of the human spirit. This will be brought about particularly by the development of modern science, which is described by Ellis as being in accordance with 'the true Greek spirit'. The five authors whom he discusses in the succeeding chapters are presented as liberators of the human spirit, and as embodiments of the successive stages of this classical renascence as they work themselves out in the moral history of mankind.

This approach, which leads Ellis to say that he is not primarily concerned with Whitman and Tolstoy 'as artists', appropriates the ideas of Bourget to an evolutionary scheme. Diderot is seen as the precursor of the synthesizing scientific spirit of the impending renascence. Heine is presented as the embodiment of the unresolved conflict between body and soul, and Whitman as the triumphant embodiment of its resolution: 'Whitman represents, for the first time since Christianity swept over the world, the re-integration . . . of the instincts of the entire man.'[32] Tolstoy represents an impending return to a form of social organization resembling that of primitive communism, whilst Ibsen is the prophet of a new race of great aristocratic individuals. 'It is only by the creation of great men and women', agrees Ellis, '. . . that

the realization of Democracy is possible.'³³ (In *Ghosts,* unlike
so many of his contemporaries, he perceives 'the hope . . .
that lies in a glad trust of nature and of natural instincts'.)

Of the various writers and artists discussed by Ellis in
The New Spirit, it is Millet and Whitman whose work has
come closest to fulfilling the ideals of this coming renascence,
which he several times describes as a return to 'the Greek
spirit':

> Millet and Whitman have . . . made the most earnest,
> thorough, and successful attempts of modern times to
> bring the Greek spirit into art. . . . It is not by the smooth
> nudities of a Bouguereau or a Leighton that we reach
> Hellenism. The Greek spirit is the simple, natural, beau-
> tiful interpretation of the life of the artist's own age and
> people under his own sky, as shown especially in the
> human body.³⁴

This classical paganism, with which Ellis associates such
terms as 'simplicity', 'wholeness' and 'health', is above all
characterized by that belief in the identity of flesh and spirit
which Diderot had proclaimed and Heine striven unsuccessfully to assert. In the eighteenth century, writes Ellis, this
'tendency' was most forcefully expressed by William Blake:
'Especially in "The Marriage of Heaven and Hell" . . . he
has set forth his conviction that "first the notion that a man
has a body distinct from his soul is to be expunged".'³⁵ Now,
and in the face of a restrictive puritanism, the tendency represented by Blake has boldly emerged in the work of Walt
Whitman, where it is most fully expressed in Whitman's
attitude towards sexual relationships. With considerable
audacity, Ellis presents this as Whitman's central moral
concern:

> This moral element is one of the central features in
> Whitman's attitude towards sex and the body generally.
> . . . 'Leaves of Grass' is penetrated by this moral element.
> How curiously far this attitude is from the old Christian

way we realize when we turn to those days in which Christianity was at its height, and see how Saint Bernard . . . looked out into the world of Nature and saw men as 'stinking spawn, sacks of dung, the food of worms.'[36]

In *Affirmations,* which was published eight years after *The New Spirit,* Ellis makes the same point with regard to Nietzsche. Passing lightly over Nietzsche's concept of master-morality, Ellis presents him in the main as one who 'desired to detach the "bad conscience" from the things that are merely wicked traditionally, and to attach it to the things that are anti-natural, anti-instinctive, anti-sensuous'. Nietzsche, he says:

> ever regarded the Greek conception of Dionysus as the key to the mystery of life. In *Götzendämmerung,* the last of his works, this is still affirmed, more distinctly than ever. 'The fundamental Hellenic instinct,' he there wrote, 'was first revealed in the Dionysiac mysteries. . . . The sexual symbol was to the Greeks the profoundest and most venerable symbol in the whole range of ancient piety. . . . Christianity alone, with its fundamental horror of life, has made sexuality an impure thing, casting filth on the beginning, the very condition of our life.'[37]

The Hellenistic dissatisfaction with nineteenth-century culture which Ellis shares with Nietzsche has led him to an increasing preference for the classical eighteenth century, as he states in his essay on Casanova in *Affirmations.* In his youth he had regarded the eighteenth century as no more than a period of stagnation and decay before the 'Easter day of the human soul' which constituted the nineteenth. Now he has gained a new admiration for the eighteenth century as the age in which the true English spirit, which is characterized by a Roman sobriety, sanity and sagacity, achieved its finest expression. The eighteenth century was one in which Christianity appeared to be decaying, and in which the 'tolerant paganism of classic days' seemed to be asserting itself robustly in England.

Decadence, so often regarded during the period as the antithesis of classicism, was not discussed by Ellis in any detail until his essay on Huysmans, which was published in *Affirmations* in 1898. Introducing Bourget's theory of deca- dence to English readers in 1889, he had merely commented that it helped to explain much in the cultural situation which Bourget had undertaken to analyse. In 1896, at the end of his article 'The Colour-Sense in Literature', he had made the extremely curious claim that his colour-test furnished no support for the prevailing notion that contemporary litera- ture was decadent. On the contrary, claimed Ellis, his test proved that the late-nineteenth-century poetic vision of the world closely resembled that of 'classic times'.

In his essay on Huysmans, Ellis discusses four types of decadence: social, artistic, moral and religious. He quotes Bourget's theory of decadence once more, and agrees with him that 'an age of individualism is usually an age of artistic decadence'. He sees no disadvantage in social decadence of this kind, however, as individualism ultimately benefits the community as a whole. Decadent art, too, has its own beauty:

> We may well reserve our finest admiration for the classic in art, for therein are included the largest and most im- posing works of human skill; but our admiration is of little worth if it is founded on incapacity to appreciate the decadent. Each has its own virtues, each is equally right and necessary.[38]

Artistic decadence, moreover, is on no account to be con- fused with moral decadence:

> We have to recognise that decadence is an aesthetic and not a moral conception. The power of words is great, but they need not befool us. The classic herring should suggest no moral superiority over the decadent bloater. We are not called upon to air our moral indignation

over the bass end of the musical clef. All confusion of intellectual substances is foolish, and one may well sympathise with that fervid unknown metaphysician to whom we owe the Athanasian creed when he went so far as to assert that it is damnable.[39]

The type of decadence which Ellis argues against most strongly is religious. Discussing what he regards as an excessive interest in supernaturalism on the part of his contemporaries, he defines decadence of this kind as the opposite of the classical paganism which he so consistently advocates by means of his critical essays:

> Pagan art and its clear serenity, science, rationalism, the bright, rough vigour of the sun and the sea, the adorable mystery of common life and commonplace human love . . . make up the spirit that in any age we call 'classic.'
>
> Thus what we call classic corresponds on the spiritual side to the love of natural things, and what we call decadent to the research for the things which seem to lie beyond Nature.[40]

The present time, says Ellis, is one in which a reaction against 'The classic party of Nature' has 'attained a certain ascendancy.' Confident that his contemporaries will eventually return to nature and to rationalism, he tolerantly advises them to 'be drunken with mediaevalism, occultism, spiritualism, theosophy, and even, if you will, protestantism—the cup that cheers, possibly, but surely not inebriates—for the satisfaction that comes of all these is good while it lasts'.[41]

In discussing the topic of decadence thus calmly, and in making important distinctions between various types of decadence, Ellis was no doubt in his essay on Huysmans attempting to assuage public hostility against all forms of decadence and degeneration, a hostility which had grown rapidly since the trial of Oscar Wilde and the publication of Nordau's *Degeneration* in 1895. He was also probably trying to disassociate himself from a movement for which, as a circulator of Lombroso's ideas, he was partly responsible. In the public mind and in the minds of the classicist cultural critics who came after him, however, notions of social, artistic and moral decadence continued to be inextricably intertwined.

In his Hellenistic campaign to free the sexual instinct, Ellis understandably complained that contemporary English authors were not permitted to discuss the sexual aspects of human experience. In his early 'A Note on Paul Bourget' he compares the restricted subject-matter of contemporary English fiction unfavourably with the freer subject-matter of French and Russian fiction. Contrasting Paul Bourget's novel *Cruelle Enigme* with *Colonel Enderby's Wife* by the English authoress 'Lucas Malet', he concludes that 'We are not likely to see in England . . . any successful union of the French and English novel, because our great English novelists have not touched the facts of life with the same frankness and boldness, and their conception of normal life is unduly restricted.'[42] What is required, says Ellis, is a type of fiction sufficiently naturalistic to allow the portrayal of the entire man:

> English novels are still for the most part what at one time French novels were, romantic; they are feebly struggling after a new ideal. We need, as it has been well said, a synthesis of naturalism and romanticism; we need to reconstitute the complete man, instead of studying him in separate pieces; to put a living soul in the clothed body. It is because they have to some extent done this that the great Russian novelists—Dostoieffsky, Tourgueneff and Tolstoi—are so significant; and Bourget, with his more limited means, seems to be striving towards the same ideal.[43]

In his earliest major literary article, published in 1883, Ellis had particularly praised Thomas Hardy for the realistic way in which his heroines were depicted. For the heroines of conventional Victorian fiction, says Ellis, sexual passion is always subservient to morality. Hardy's women, however, are 'creatures . . . made up of more or less untamed instincts for both love and admiration, who can never help some degree of response when the satisfaction of those instincts lies open to them'.[44] Thirteen years later, writing on *Jude the Obscure* in *The Savoy,* he defends Hardy's novel against the cries of 'morbidity' and 'immorality' which had greeted its publication in 1895 (which was, of course, the year of *Degeneration*). Ellis considers *Jude* to be the greatest novel written in England for many years. It is concerned with the realities of married life, which the romantic fiction of court-ship never discusses, and it embodies, not a specific moral lesson, but that conflict between nature and society, between 'passion' and 'law', which Ellis regards as an essential part of life and of any work of art which deals honestly with life. In this same essay Ellis states that as far as the nineteenth century is concerned, he now finds greatness only in the French and Russian novel. The great tradition of the Eng-lish eighteenth-century novel, he says, has never recovered from the baneful influence of Sir Walter Scott, who by means of his enormous reputation 'was enabled to debase the intel-lectual and moral currency in this department of literature to the lowest possible limit', and who 'threw the English novel into disorganisation from which it has not even to-day recovered'.[45]

Ellis's attack upon the evasiveness of Victorian fiction is pressed home in his essay on Zola, which also appeared in *The Savoy,* and which was later reprinted in *Affirmations.* 'All our great poets and novelists from Chaucer to Fielding', writes Ellis, 'wrote sincerely and heroically concerning the great facts of life.' In the nineteenth century, however, liter-ary exploration has given way to commercial exploration, with the result that contemporary English literature has become parochial and infantile:

> In our own age and country daring has passed out of the channels of art into those of commerce, to find exercise,

foolish enough sometimes, in the remotest corners of the
earth. It is because our literature is not heroic, but has
been confined within the stifling atmosphere of the
drawing-room, that English poets and novelists have
ceased to be a power in the world and are almost unknown outside the parlours and nurseries of our own
country.[46]

Zola is praised by Ellis for having extended the range of
literary language and the range of the novelist's subject-
matter. Zola, he says, has restored to the novel its freedom
to deal with the 'central functions of life' which is essential
to great literature. He concedes that Zola has to some extent
'missed the restraint of well-balanced art' in his treatment
of the sexual and digestive functions, but defends him against
charges of prurience and coprolalia by claiming that there
are far worse cases in literature, where 'their most pronounced exponents have been clerics, the conventional representa-
tives of the Almighty'. In these respects, says Ellis, Zola has
'by no means come up with Father Rabelais and Dean Swift
and the Rev. Laurence Sterne'.[47] These remarks are almost
certainly intended as a rejoinder to Nordau, who was cur-
rently encouraging the literary censorship which Ellis opposed by teaching the British public that 'M. Zola is affected
by coprolalia to a very high degree', and that the fact of
Zola's being 'a sexual psychopath is betrayed on every page
of his novels'.[48]

Hellenistic nostalgia for pagan simplicity during the nineteenth century goes hand in hand with disdain for indus-
trialization and commercialism, and it is for these topics that
Ellis reserves his sharpest and least ambiguous tone. In the
introduction to *The New Spirit* he complains that 'The
fanatical commercialism that has filled so much of our century made art impossible', but takes comfort from the fact
that England is losing her commercial supremacy. 'There
will soon be no reason', he notes with satisfaction, 'why the
coarse products of a great part of the earth should be sent

all the way to a small northern country to be returned in
a more or less ugly and adulterate manufactured condition.'
These attitudes are intensified in *Affirmations,* which has as
a dominant motif the ideal of 'fine living' from which men
are barred by the material and mechanical 'triumphs' of the
Victorian era. The English, says Ellis, have hitherto been
characterized by their restless activity and their neglect of
the sensory aspects of life, and the impending commercial
decline of England is to be welcomed rather than feared.
'The Japanese masses', he remarks, 'who fix their popular
festival for the day when the cherry-tree is in finest bloom
. . . may possibly not succeed in sending ugly and shoddy
goods to clothe and kill the beautiful skins of every savage
tribe under heaven, but we need not fear to affirm that
they have learnt secrets of civilisation which are yet hidden
from us in England.'[49] Having described the splendid
achievements of the previous century, he concludes that:

> Men will scarcely look back to our own century as so
> good to live in. One may well say that he would have
> gladly lived in the thirteenth century, perhaps the most
> interesting of all since Christ, or in the sixteenth, prob-
> ably the most alive of all, or in the eighteenth, surely
> the most human. But why have lived in the nineteenth,
> the golden age of machinery, and of men used as
> machines?[50]

Ellis's critique of Victorian commercialism was continued
and extended in *The Nineteenth Century: A Dialogue in
Utopia,* which was published in 1900. Provoked by the frequently expressed view that the century just ended was 'the
most wonderful century that up to then the world had seen',
he expressed his disapproval in a manner more direct and
polemical than hitherto. It was commercialism, according
to Ellis, which underlay both the follies of the century and
the self-deceptions by which it sought to conceal them. Commercialism was taken to be civilization itself: 'At one moment
in the nineteenth century the English found themselves at

the head in wealth, in steam power, in shipping, in manu-
facture, in railways; they imagined all that was "civilisation";
they were happy and satisfied.' Such civilization as the Vic-
torians possessed, however, was dedicated not to creation but
to destruction:

> If it was a matter of killing other people, they were
> admirably organised, and could mobilise enormous de-
> structive powers at a moment's notice. If it was a matter
> of preserving life or of making life beautiful, they had
> no national organisation of any importance, and fell back
> into individualistic chaos. But what motive had they to
> do otherwise? The birth-rate was high, and they had no
> thirst for beauty.[51]

The same commercialism which underlay imperialism,
arrogant nationalism and military violence was also responsible for the spread of journalism, of mass-produced opinion,
and consequently of the herd-instinct:

> The chief occupation being a scramble for the vacant
> places of the earth's surface and fighting with other na-
> tions, it was necessary to rely chiefly on uniform machine-
> made goods and uniform machine-made thoughts. This
> latter important commodity was in some departments
> supplied by the social machinery of their lives, and in
> other departments by the well-organised machinery of
> journalism.[52]

Commercialism, finally, was responsible for the spread of
ugliness and the decay of literature, architecture, and the
plastic arts:

> In earlier ages, when men needed few things, they
> naturally had time and energy to make these few things
> beautiful—that is to say, to mould them into those shapes
> which alone satisfy the organic demands of their nature.
> But at this time they suddenly acquired a passion for
> desiring many things without any corresponding aptitude
> to attain beauty at an equally rapid rate. Consequently

all their things were ugly. Of all ages in the world's history that was, indeed, the one which shows the least trace of the art instinct.[53]

The Nineteenth Century is in the form of a dialogue between two men who are looking back on Victorian society from a period in the remote future. This narrative technique produces an effect of distance which reinforces the prevailing tone of coolly detached irony. Tone and technique together bespeak Ellis's evolutionary confidence that the twentieth century will be one in which Hellenistic classicism will triumph, and nineteenth-century sexual repression, literary censorship and commercialism wither away.

iv

'To-day', writes Ellis in 1890, '. . . we stand, as it were, at the beginning of a new era',[54] and there is little doubt that he speaks here for the majority of his contemporaries in the Age of Evolutionism. Yeats's account of the 'tragic generation' is highly persuasive, but it is probably as well to remember that its author was dedicated to the construction of public myths out of private experiences. More generally reliable than Yeats's account of the 1890s is that of Holbrook Jackson, especially when he draws attention to the use of the word 'New' during the period:

> Anything strange or uncanny, anything which savoured of freak or perversity, was swiftly labelled *fin-de-siècle,* and given a certain topical prominence. . . . But side by side with the prevailing use of the phrase, and running its popularity very close, came the adjective 'new' . . . The range of the adjective gradually spread until it embraced the ideas of the whole period, and we find innumerable references to the 'New Spirit', the 'New Humour', . . . and the 'New Woman'.[55]

Jackson overlooks an essential distinction, however, when he writes that both *'fin-de-siècle'* and 'New' were 'applied in much the same way to indicate extreme modernity'. *'Fin-de-*

siècle' was mostly used, as by Nordau, to describe the decadent products of a society in decline. The word 'New' was applied to whatever had, in a spirit of evolutionary optimism, decisively turned its back upon this 'effete and degenerating culture' as Ellis calls it in *The New Spirit,* this 'spiritually barren and exhausted age' as he calls it in *Affirmations.*

Seen from the point of view of the history of literature and of literary criticism, Ellis is undeniably a figure of major importance, especially as an innovator. He wrote the first full-length introductions in English to the work of Nietzsche and Huysmans, edited the first English collection of Ibsen's plays, and launched Bourget's theory of decadence upon its English career. He also drew early attention to the work of such Russian authors as Turgenev, Gogol and Dostoievsky, and such Scandinavian authors as Brandes and Björnson. Employing his own seminal ideas, together with those of Bourget and possibly Freud, he attempted to introduce the methods of psychology into literary criticism. Employing the ideas of Galton and Lombroso, he attempted to introduce the methods of anthropology. In the face of hysterical hostility he defended and discussed the work of Zola, Hardy, Whitman and Tolstoy, as well as Nietzsche, Huysmans and Ibsen, describing these authors as moral and religious teachers at a time when Zola's English publisher had recently been prosecuted and when Nordau had persuaded many that they were degenerates to a man.

Seen from the point of view of the history of ideas, Ellis is interesting and important in two main ways. Firstly, he reflects the 'New' world-view brought about by evolutionary theories of history and the sheer growth of scientific and historical information during the late nineteenth century. One of the distinguishing features of this new world-view is its awareness of the old, and Ellis's generation differs from its predecessors not only in its evolutionary dynamism but in its panoramic sense of history, its relativistic awareness of other systems of religion, morality and culture, and its encyclopaedic ambitions for ideological synthesis. Havelock

Ellis inhabits a conceptual world so different from that of Matthew Arnold, for example, that a reader of *The New Spirit* will find it difficult to remember that the second series of Arnold's *Essays in Criticism* had been published no more than two years earlier.

Secondly, Ellis displays three important characteristics of evolutionary thinking. The first of these is his keen interest in the factors necessary to produce a new race of men of genius; the second is his use of modern scientific notions to rehabilitate thoroughly traditional ideals, such as those of Hellenism. The third and most important characteristic is his attempt to formulate a unified view of man and the universe to replace that of a Christianity regarded as no longer tenable. In making this attempt Ellis relies upon biological assumptions. 'We know at last', he writes in *The New Spirit* concerning mankind's future progress, 'that it must be among our chief ethical rules to see that we build the lofty structure of human society on the sure and simple foundations of man's organism.'[56]

For Ellis, man is an organism possessed of three basic instincts: the sexual instinct, the artistic instinct, and the instinct for religious mysticism. The satisfaction of these instincts constitutes wholeness, and Ellis's criticism, as we have seen, is always directed against whatever frustrates the human drive towards wholeness.

As a pioneer in the application of psychology to literary criticism Ellis paved the way for I. A. Richards, C. K. Ogden, and those who applied Freud's theories to literature. As an apologist of 'the whole man alive', opposing Manichaeism and Manichaean restrictions upon the subject-matter of literature, he appears to stand at the beginning of a movement which finds its fullest expression in the work of D. H. Lawrence. As a critic of commercialism, in his rejection of nineteenth-century literature in favour of eighteenth-century literature, and in his preference for the classical over the decadent, he anticipated much that was to appear in extremer forms in *The New Age* a decade later.

3

The Art of Modernity
Arthur Symons

Arthur William Symons was born at Milford Haven in Wales in 1865, the year of Yeats's birth. His father was a Wesleyan minister whose frequent changes of appointment caused the family to move house often during Symons's childhood and adolescence. Most of these appointments were to circuits in Devon and Cornwall, though some took the family to Northumberland and the Midlands.

Of the three critics discussed in this book only Symons devoted his energies entirely to literature and the arts. He chose a literary career early, and during a long working life produced an extremely large number of poems, plays, stories, translations, anthologies, editions, prefaces, reviews, articles and collections of essays. By the age of twenty-five he had already edited a volume of Leigh Hunt's essays, two volumes of Massinger's plays (for Havelock Ellis's Mermaid series), and four volumes of Furnivall's *Shakspere Quarto Fac-Similes,* besides working on eight plays in *The Henry Irving Shakespeare.* He had made several contributions to the *Browning Society Papers,* published articles in leading periodicals on Meredith, Pater, Mistral, Villiers de l'Isle-Adam and Odilon Redon, published his first book of criticism (*An Introduction to the Study of Browning*) and his first book of verse (*Days and Nights*). He had gained the friendship of Walter Pater and Coventry Patmore, and in company with Havelock Ellis had made the acquaintance of Verlaine, Mallarmé, and the leading Symbolist poets and painters in Paris. He had also edited *The Academy* for a few weeks. As he maintained this tempo until 1908, when his sanity was severely impaired, there is space here for no more than the merest outline of his subsequent career.

Symons made London his home in 1891, living in Fountain Court in the Temple until his marriage ten years later. In 1891 he joined the regular staff of *The Athenaeum* and in 1892 became the music-hall and ballet critic of *The Star*. In 1891 he joined the Rhymers' Club, and in 1892 published his second book of verse, *Silhouettes*. His third book of verse, *London Nights,* met with considerable hostility because of its Decadent eroticism, as might be expected of a work published in the same year as Nordau's *Degeneration*. During these years Symons continued to publish essays and reviews, especially on the work of contemporary French authors.

In late 1895 and early 1896 Yeats stayed with Symons, in the rooms at Fountain Court usually occupied by Havelock Ellis, and in the summer of 1896 the two visited Ireland together. At the end of this year, during which Symons was editing *The Savoy,* he travelled to Italy, where he met Gabriele D'Annunzio and the actress Eléonora Duse. In the following year he and Havelock Ellis visited Moscow. Travelling by way of Bayreuth, they attended a performance of *Parsifal* which appears to have profoundly affected Symons's outlook.

Brought up in a strict Nonconformist household, Symons had lost his religious faith during adolescence. Partly as a result of his closer acquaintance with Yeats, he turned increasingly towards mysticism during 1896 and 1897. Signs of this appear in his first collection of critical essays, *Studies in Two Literatures* (1897), while *The Symbolist Movement in Literature* of 1899 is amongst other things a public declaration of conversion.

After 1900 Symons's criticism took a decidely expressionist and Nietzschean turn. This is most apparent in his *William Blake* (1907), but almost completely obscured by the miscellaneous nature of such collections as *Plays, Acting, and*

Music (1903, revised edition 1909), *Studies in Verse and Prose* (1904), and *Studies in Seven Arts* (1906).

In late 1908, when he was still no more than forty-three years old, Symons suffered a severe nervous breakdown which led to his confinement in a mental hospital. He never completely recovered, although he returned home in 1910 and continued to write and translate until his death in 1945. His later poetry is often tormented, and his later essays often a pathetic collage of paragraphs from the writings of his prime. His work after his breakdown is without relevance to his achievement as a critic.

I shall suggest that this achievement was considerable. Whatever our final estimate of Symons's stature as a critic, however, it will already be evident that his lingering reputation as a Decadent trifler is entirely undeserved. He was clearly a man of extraordinary restlessness, energy, creativity and originality.

ii

When we read Symons's criticism in the order in which it appeared in periodicals, it becomes clear that between 1885 and 1908 it went through three main stages of development. Although each stage evolved gradually from the one before, we can conveniently distinguish an impressionist phase ending about 1893, a symbolist phase ending about 1900, and an expressionist phase ending in 1908. In some ways, as in his recurrent antipathy to 'description' in the arts, Symons's criticism changed but little between 1885 and 1908. In other ways it changed radically, so that his critical estimates of 1907, say, differ considerably from those of ten years before. During the early years of the twentieth century the tone of his criticism became steadily harsher, and on the eve of his breakdown he had rejected nearly all the figures for whom he had campaigned during the 1890s. In the first section of this chapter I consider the impressionist phase of his criticism, which culminated in his well-known essay of 1893, 'The Decadent Movement in Literature'.

The topic of decadence, which is far less important in Symons's criticism than in Ellis's and Orage's, may be disposed of at once. The salient facts are these. Between 1889 and 1893 Symons in his criticism very occasionally used phrases which were Decadent in the sense that with an air of approval they associated the diseased with the erotic in literature. In 1892, for example, he described one of Verlaine's sonnets as 'the most delirious and depraved bit of verse imaginable',[1] and in the following year he applauded D'Annunzio's 'marvellous, malarious *Piacere*' as 'a triumph of exquisite perversity'.[2] At the same time, however, Symons was in the habit of dismissing the followers of Verlaine and Huysmans in such Lombroso-like terms as 'the noisy little school of *Décadents*' and 'the brainsick little school of *Symbolistes*'.[3] Describing Huysmans's *A Rebours* as 'the quintessence of contemporary Decadence', he was careful to add that there was 'a danger of being too much attracted, or too much repelled'[4] by the singular qualities of Huysmans's writing.

In 1896 Symons announced a forthcoming book to be entitled *The Decadent Movement in Literature*,[5] although he had already perceived in Alfred Jarry's play *Ubu Roi* the end of this movement.[6] This book, which was to have contained essays on Verlaine, the brothers Goncourt, Huysmans, Villiers and Maeterlinck, did not appear, but evidently formed the basis of *The Symbolist Movement in Literature*, which was published three years later. By 1897 Symons had limited the meaning of the term 'decadence' to 'that learned corruption of language by which style ceases to be organic',[7] and in 1898, when he described the work of the poet Baudelaire and the artists Aubrey Beardsley and Félicien Rops as 'great decadent art', he apologized for this as 'really a sacrifice to the eternal beauty, and only seemingly to the powers of evil'.[8] In 1899 Symons dismissed the entire Decadent movement as 'half a mock-interlude'[9] before the dawn of symbolism, and until his breakdown nearly ten years later rarely mentioned decadence again. This said, we may begin our survey of the genuinely important aspects of Symons's criticism.

Between 1885 (when he was twenty years of age) and 1890, modern poetry was represented for Symons by the work of Browning and Meredith. The qualities which most interested him in their work were their avoidance of stereotyped diction and subject-matter, their pursuit of exact expression, their experimental approach to language, and their attempts to communicate states of mind which were modern in their complexity. The young Symons was above all interested in the ability of these writers to 'flash images' directly to the reader's mind, thus side-stepping what he called 'description'.

'The poetry of mere description', writes Symons in his first book of criticism, his *Introduction to the Study of Browning* (1886), 'is of all verse the dreariest and the most inept.'[10] The aim of the writer, he agrees with Meredith, should be to rouse the reader's 'inward vision'. The writer should not describe a scene in detail, in other words, but find a means of duplicating it in the reader's mind. Nor should the external world be described simply for its own sake. The landscapes which Browning sees 'with instant and intense clearness, and stamps . . . as clearly on our brain' are not ends in themselves, according to the young Symons, but a means of communicating to the reader the emotional states experienced by his characters: 'The picture calls up the mood.'[11] The pictorial image is a means of duplicating, in the reader's mind, the mood in the narrator's mind.

In 1890, reviewing Browning's posthumous *Asolando: Facts and Fancies,* Symons summed up his position by stating that only Heine, Browning and Meredith 'have succeeded in dealing, in a tone of what I may call sympathetic irony, with the unheroic complications of modern life—so full of poetic matter really, but of matter so difficult to handle'.[12] In this same review, however, he makes the first of his many later references to Verlaine's advocacy of 'la Nuance', of suggestion rather than statement, and his criticism of the next two years shows that he had found in other writers besides Browning and Meredith the type of modernity for which he was searching.

In 1886 Symons had praised the Provençal poet Mistral for being untouched by 'the mean conditions of town-life, so entirely destructive of poetry'.[13] In 1891, however, reviewing George Moore's *Impressions and Opinions,* he commends especially Moore's study of Degas, 'the painter who has created a new art, ultra-modern, *fin-de-siècle,* the art of the ballet, the bathroom, the washing-tub, the racecourse, the shop-window',[14] and in his major article of 1892 on Verlaine he puts forward Verlaine's expression of 'the tumultuous impressions . . . of . . . the modern man of cities'[15] as an important element of his modernism. In the same year, reviewing W. E. Henley's *The Song of the Sword,* he proposed 'the capacity for dealing with London' as the crucial test of modern poetry, and described Henley's book as a notable manifesto on behalf of the art of modernity in poetry. He regards the 'London Voluntaries' and certain of the 'Rhymes and Rhythms' ('In Hospital') as the most successfully modern of Henley's poems, and having quoted from the first of the 'London Voluntaries' he takes the painting of Whistler, as so often in the future, for his touchstone:

> Is not this . . . almost as fine as Whistler?—instinct with the same sense of the poetry of cities, the romance of what lies beneath our eyes, if we only have the vision and the point of view. Here, at last, is a poet who can so enlarge the limits of his verse as to take in London. And I think that might be the test of poetry which professes to be really modern—its capacity for dealing with London, with what one sees or might see there, indoors or out.

He refers to the achievements of contemporary *painters,* once again, in order to justify the unusual subject-matter of the 'half-physiological' poetry of the 'In Hospital' sequence, referring to a painting by Whistler which is usually known as 'The Falling Rocket':

> It is one of the modern discoveries that the 'dignity of the subject' is a mere figure of speech, and a misleading one. See what Mr. Whistler can make out of 'Brock's Benefit:' in place of fireworks and vulgarity you have a harmony of black and gold, and a work of art. See what Degas can discover for you in the crossing of colours, the violent rhythm of movements, the crowded and empty spaces of a ballet rehearsal. And so, instead of prattling about Phyllis, Mr. Henley has set himself to the task of rendering the more difficult poetry of the disagreeable.[16]

While he applauds Henley's poetry as 'always insistently modern, with such fine use of "hansoms," of "fifth-floor windows"', Symons makes it clear that the main use of these elements of the urban scene is to communicate the modern poet's inner experiences, and he praises Henley for the variety of subjective moods and emotions which his poetry expresses. Even the best contemporary verse, he says, is characterized by a bourgeois solemnity, while Henley's is 'casual as one's moods, sensations, caprices'. He cannot fully approve of some of Henley's unrhymed 'Rhythms', however, and cites the example of Verlaine in support of his view:

> But to do without rhyme is to do without one of the beauties of poetry, I should say one of the inherent beauties. . . . The example of the French Décadents should be a warning to those in England who are anxious to loosen the bonds of verse. . . . Yet the really great, the really modern poet of France—the leader, as they would fain hail him, of the noisy little school of *Décadents,* the brainsick little school of *Symbolistes,* has always held aloof from these extravagances.[17]

Symons's review is itself 'a notable manifesto on behalf of . . . the art of modernity in poetry', and a far more important document in the history of modern poetry than his better-known essay, 'The Decadent Movement in Literature', of 1893. The real import of that misleadingly entitled essay must be considered, however, before I bring together the main points of the extremely modern poetic which Symons had developed between 1885 and 1893.

Under the heading of the Decadent Movement, Symons groups well over a dozen writers, of whom the most unlikely bedfellows are Pater and Ibsen. Although he begins by suggesting that 'The most representative literature of the day . . . has all the qualities . . . that we find in the Greek, the Latin, decadence', he soon makes it clear that by Decadents he means either impressionists or symbolists, and that he himself is interested mainly in the impressionists. Both impressionists and symbolists, he says, 'are really working on the same hypothesis, applied in different directions. What both seek is not general truth merely, but *la vérité vraie*, the very essence of truth . . .' The impressionist seeks 'the truth of the appearances to the senses', while the symbolist seeks 'the truth of spiritual things to the spiritual vision'. Both, in short, aim at a wholly exact rendering of particular experiences, whether sensory or spiritual, and their search for exactness has led both to discard stereotyped modes of expression:

> And naturally, necessarily, this endeavor after a perfect truth to one's impression, to one's intuition—perhaps an impossible endeavor—has brought with it, in its revolt from ready-made impressions and conclusions, a revolt from the ready-made of language, from the bondage of traditional form, of a form become rigid.[18]

What Symons finds to praise in Mallarmé, whom at this time he otherwise mocks, is that he has endowed the French language with 'new capacities for the exact noting of sensation'. And it is to this impressionist capacity for the exact and direct rendering of the impressions of the physical senses that he continually returns in this essay. Henley's 'London

Voluntaries', he says, 'flash before us certain aspects of the poetry of London as only Whistler had ever done', while the search of the brothers Goncourt for *l'image peinte* is 'a desperate endeavor to give sensation, to flash the impression of the moment, to preserve the very heat and motion of life'.[19]

'The Decadent Movement in Literature' is not in fact about Decadence but about impressionism, and 'The Impressionist Movement in Literature' would have been a far better choice of title. Its greatest value is probably to emphasize that Symons equates impressionism not with vagueness but with unprecedented accuracy and immediacy of communication. It also serves to remind us however that he was no slavish follower of French fashions, but one who was to find in contemporary French literature what he had already been in search of for several years. The basic concerns of the essay on the Decadent Movement are already evident in Symons's 'Note on Browning and Meredith' of 1885. Both of these authors, he says there, 'seem to experience a like irritation at the inevitable boundaries of words', and sometimes strain the language to uncouthness in their search for exact expression. When their search for exact expression is successful, few others 'can so flash an image on us in a word or phrase'.[20] This notion of the 'flashed image', which is not uncommon in Symons's earliest criticism, perhaps derives from the magic-lantern: 'Brilliant and fantastically lighted pictures flit past', he writes in connection with Meredith's *The Adventures of Harry Richmond,* 'like the slides of a magic-lantern.'[21]

The main aim of the modern writer, to sum up the views expressed by Symons between 1885 and 1893, was to make new areas of human experience available to literature, especially to poetry. Modern poetry should be capable of representing the complex inner life of man in the modern city. It should be free to communicate the shifting and diverse moods of the poet, and to employ subject-matter previously regarded as undignified and disagreeable. It should be casual rather than solemn in its attitudes, and its tone should be complex and ironic. These aims required a revolution in poetic techniques. Poets should experiment with language in order to communicate, as accurately as possible, complex combinations of emotional moods, physical sensations, and visual impressions. They must disregard stereotyped expressions and conventional poetic diction: Verlaine's words are 'now *récherché,* now confidently common-place—words of the boudoir, words of the street!'[22] They must also create new and unconventional rhythms, though without taking the ultimate step of writing in *vers libres.* These developments in technique would make possible a poetry which would not simply describe an experience, but would be so subtle and complex in its operations and resources as to be able to 'flash' *the experience itself* with unprecedented accuracy and immediacy to the mind of the reader.

Symons's own short poem 'Going to Hammersmith' is a good example of what he was aiming at during his period of urban impressionism. Written in 1891, this poem was afterwards re-titled 'In the Train':

> The train through the night of the town,
>   Through a blackness broken in twain
>   By the sudden finger of streets;
> Lights, red, yellow, and brown,
>   From curtain and window-pane,
>   The flashing eyes of the streets.
>
> Night, and the rush of the train,
>   A cloud of smoke through the town,
>   Scaring the life of the streets;
> And the leap of the heart again,
>   Out into the night, and down
>   The dazzling vista of streets![23]

There is nothing conventionally poetic here. The subject-matter concerns everyday urban experience and the diction is extremely plain. There is no intention of conveying a grand emotion or an improving message. The poem is deliberately

slight. Yet its techniques reveal a serious and novel attempt
at the simultaneous communication of simultaneous mental
events. Symons excludes finite verbs, as these would impose
a temporal sequence upon the poem, and he knits the
poem together by repeating rhyme-words in such a way
that it continually turns back upon itself. There is no narrative progression, and the details of the journey are described
not for their own sakes but as a means of communicating
the poet's feelings of excitement and adventure. These themselves are not described. Instead: 'The picture calls up the
mood.' Symons is attempting, in short, to evoke his own
multi-faceted emotionally charged 'impression' as a single
instantaneous experience in the mind of the reader. Or, as
Pound was to put it later, to present to the reader 'an intellectual and emotional complex in an instant of time'.

Symons's views of this period clearly anticipate several
basic tenets of early-twentieth-century poetic theory and
practice, so much so that T. S. Eliot's 'Prufrock', except in
the matter of its length, might be regarded as fulfilling
several of his precepts to the letter. The similarities between
Symons's impressionist poetic and that of the imagist poets
will be discussed in more detail at the end of the present
chapter. For the moment I turn my attention to the way in
which Symons, having ranged himself on the side of the
impressionists up to the time of his essay on the Decadent
Movement, became a convert to symbolism and mysticism.

iii

Although Symons did not publicly declare his interest in
mysticism until 1896, three unsigned articles of 1893 and
1895 show that he was considerably interested in religion
and mysticism before he became more closely involved with
Yeats after 1895. In 1893, reviewing Coventry Patmore's
Religio Poetae, he ranked Patmore highly as a poet and drew
particular attention to his mysticism,[24] while in his obituary
article of 1895 on Christina Rossetti he praised her religious

poems especially.[25] Later in 1895 he praised *En Route,* the novel in which Huysmans describes his own religious conversion, for its subtle investigation of those intellectual and religious passions which are 'as varied and tumultuous as those of the heart'.[26]

Patmore, whom Symons had known from 1885, appears to have strongly influenced him in the direction of mysticism. In 1895, the year in which Patmore died, Symons published a signed article on him which talks freely of the lady of *The Unknown Eros* as 'the mystical rose of beauty . . . the Madonna',[27] and in 1897 this article and the originally anonymous article on Christina Rossetti were published in *Studies in Two Literatures.* Reviewing Maeterlinck's *Le Trésor des Humbles* in 1897, Symons makes it clear that he has already arrived at the central argument of *The Symbolist Movement in Literature*: science and positivism have shown themselves to be bankrupt, and are now giving way to 'the mystical doctrine'.[28] In 1898 he made his change of heart still more apparent by publishing an edition of *The Confessions of St. Augustine.*

'I speak often in this book of Mysticism', writes Symons, dedicating *The Symbolist Movement in Literature* to Yeats, and his conclusion refers us again to 'the doctrine of Mysticism, with which all this symbolical literature has so much to do'. Putting the matter rather more plainly than Symons himself, what symbolist literature and mysticism have to do with each other is this: mysticism has deposed a bankrupt scientific materialism as the dominant European philosophy, and a major sign of this radical change is that symbolism has deposed realism as the dominant European literary movement. The previous age, of which Taine was the type-figure, was according to Symons 'the age of Science, the age of material things'. It was therefore the age of realism in literature, when words 'did miracles in the exact representation of everything that visibly existed, exactly as it existed'. From this period of science and realism, art has finally returned, by way of the 'half a mock-interlude of Decadence', to the one pathway of symbolism:

> after the world has starved its soul long enough in the contemplation and the re-arrangement of material things, comes the turn of the soul; and with it comes the literature of which I write in this volume, a literature in which the visible world is no longer a reality, and the unseen world no longer a dream.[29]

The symbolist movement, in short, is an attempt to spiritualize literature and to free it from the bondage of materialism.

Symons presents most of the authors considered in the book as committed mystics, each of whom has in his own way realized the 'central secret' of mysticism. This central secret, as Symons makes clear in his essay on Nerval, is the occult doctrine that nature is a 'sensitive unity', that every created thing possesses spiritual life and shares in the universal consciousness. 'Tout est sensible', as Nerval says in 'Vers dorés'. Or, more elaborately, in *Le Rêve et la Vie*: 'All things live, all things are in motion, all things correspond . . .' This, says Symons, is the

> central secret of the mystics, from Pythagoras onwards, the secret which the Smaragdine Tablet of Hermes betrays in its 'As things are below, so are they above'; which Boehme has classed in his teaching of 'signatures,' and Swedenborg has systematised in his doctrine of 'correspondences' . . .

It matters little, suggests Symons, that it was by means of the 'fatal initiation of madness'[30] that Nerval arrived at this greatest of secrets.

In his personal conclusion Symons suggests that mysticism satisfies our need for something 'which makes it worth while to go on living . . . at our finest intensity'. It liberates us by making us familiar with the mysteriousness of life and by teaching us to disregard the world of appearances. It brings our instincts for religion, love and art into unity with each other and the spiritual universe: 'On this theory alone', says Symons, 'does all life become worth living, all art worth making, all worship worth offering.'

Although there is evidence in *The Symbolist Movement in Literature* of Symons's familiarity with Plotinus, the type of mysticism which informs his conclusion is that of quietism, and the strongest influence that of Maeterlinck. Action is insignificant, according to Symons, and we are to delight in 'feeling ourselves carried onward by forces which it is our wisdom to obey'. In this, as in his rejection of the world of everyday appearances, Symons's mysticism is quite distinct from that of Ellis. It serves, however, the same general function as the latter's Hellenism, bringing our instincts for religion, love and art into unity with each other.

Though the tone of Symons's conclusion is restrained, it should be emphasized that *The Symbolist Movement in Literature* as a whole is a highly optimistic book. It announces the overthrow of science and materialism and proclaims 'the turn of the soul', and in his dedication Symons describes the symbolist revolt as one which is in the process of conquering all the nations of Europe. In the present chapter I mention Symons's extensive criticism of the other arts only in passing; it should be noted however that in writing about the arts other than literature, which he did increasingly after the turn of the century, Symons is often equally enthusiastic and optimistic. In 1902, for example, writing on Rodin (who believes in 'that doctrine of correspondences which lies at the root of most of the mystical teaching'), he concludes that 'even sculpture has gone the way of all the other arts, and has learnt to suggest more than it says, to embody dreams in its flesh, to become at once a living thing and a symbol'.[31] The art of the actress Eléonora Duse, he writes in 1900:

> is like the art of Verlaine in French poetry; always suggestion, never statement, always a renunciation. It comes into the movement of all the arts, as they seek to escape

from the bondage of form, by a new, finer mastery of
form, wrought outwards from within, not from without
inwards. And it conquers almost the last obstacle, as it
turns the one wholly external art, based upon mere imitation, existing upon the commonest terms of illusion,
triumphing by exaggeration, into an art wholly subtle,
almost spiritual, a suggestion, an evasion, a secrecy.[32]

For Symons the symbolist movement is above all a liberation movement. It comes to liberate the arts from what he
frequently refers to as the 'bondage' of materialism. 'It is
all an attempt to spiritualise literature', he writes in the introduction to *The Symbolist Movement in Literature,* 'to
evade the old bondage of rhetoric, the old bondage of exteriority.' In this statement, however, Symons noticeably
connects two topics which are not necessarily related to each
other. By 'rhetoric' he means grandiloquence in poetry, and
by 'exteriority' he means realism in the drama and the novel.
As far as literature is concerned his symbolist movement is
in fact not one revolt, but two. In what follows I discuss
these topics separately, referring to a number of essays besides those contained in *The Symbolist Movement in Literature.*

Symons's fundamental quarrel with realism is that it depicts only what is externally observable about man and
nature, and excludes the interior world of the mind and the
spirit. The literature of the age of science, he says in the
introduction to *The Symbolist Movement in Literature,* was
concerned with the exact representation of everything that
visibly existed. The world of the brothers Goncourt 'existed
only as a thing of flat spaces, and angles, and coloured movement', while Zola 'tried to build in brick and mortar inside
the covers of a book'. Introducing the English translation of
D'Annunzio's *Il Piacere* in 1898, Symons says that the great
exterior novels have now been written, and that what re-
mains to be explored is 'the hidden, inner self',[33] the soul of
the characters.

Huysmans has achieved this, he tells us in *The Symbolist Movement in Literature,* by converting the novel into 'the revelation of . . . the soul'. Huysmans, he tells us in the second edition of this work, has found words for 'the most subtle and illusive [*sic*] aspects of . . . inner life',[34] and the novel, which has hitherto been concerned with worldly affairs, is now 'liberated from the bondage of a too realistic conversation' and 'internalised to a complete liberty'. He defends Balzac in an important essay of 1899 as a poetic visionary to whom the word 'realism' was an insult, and who 'seeks the soul' in all that he writes of life.[35]

When he turns his attention to drama, Symons attacks realism of dialogue, realism of acting, and realism of décor. He praises Villiers de l'Isle-Adam's *Axël,* in *The Symbolist Movement in Literature,* as a Symbolist 'drama of the soul' which is written in an ideal and unrealistic language. 'It is evident', he says, 'that the average man can articulate only a small enough part of what he obscurely thinks or feels' in his soul. The theory of realism in the drama, however, 'is that his emotions and ideas are to be given only in so far as the words at his own command can give them'.

Realistic drama with its realistic dialogue can imitate only the non-essentials of human experience, he argues in his essay 'Ballet, Pantomime, and Poetic Drama' (1898), while both mime and poetic drama are in their different ways far more faithful to the fundamental realities of human experience.[36] This point is made more succinctly in the second edition of *Plays Acting and Music* (1909), where Symons claims that 'Verse lends itself to the lifting and adequate treatment of the primary emotions, because it can render them more as they are in the soul, not being tied down to probable words, as prose talk is.'[37]

In this same volume Ibsen is attacked because his 'only too probable people speak a language exactly on the level of their desks and their shop-counters',[38] which Symons describes elsewhere as 'the language of the newspaper, recorded with the fidelity of the phonograph'.[39] When verse is used in drama it must not be merely decorative, however. It must be organic, as Symons makes clear when he compares the poetic drama of Stephen Philips unfavourably with that of D'Annunzio,[40] or praises *The Countess Cathleen* of W. B. Yeats because 'the verse is organic, and grows out of the structure of the piece'.[41]

In *The Symbolist Movement in Literature* Symons praises Maeterlinck for having invented a type of drama 'so precise, so curt, so arbitrary in its limits, that it can safely be confided to the masks and feigned voices of marionettes'. He was in fact so opposed to realism in the field of acting that he was entirely willing to replace human actors by marionettes. In his 'Apology for Puppets' (1897) he argues that the expression of the human soul, which will constitute 'the drama of the future', is best achieved by the use of puppets. Like the masks of Greek drama, puppets permit the expression of the 'universal voice' and the 'great passions' of the soul of humanity, and it may be instructive for us to consider, he perceptively remarks, 'that we could not give a play of Ibsen's to marionettes, but that we could give them the "Agamemnon" '.[42]

When he wrote this Symons had behind him 'the one really satisfying performance' he had ever seen in a theatre: *Parsifal* at Bayreuth in 1897. *Parsifal,* he writes, possesses that 'hieratic character which it is the effort of supreme art to attain', and he praises the acting and staging of Wagner's opera because they possess 'the beauty of convention'. There was, he says, 'none of that base, tricky realism, which would have us believe too prosaically in the real existence of what is going on before us'. Instead, reality was re-ordered by selection and convention to form 'a new, abstract beauty'.[43] For the same reason Symons later welcomed Gordon Craig's 'new art of the stage' in London. Instead of imitating real surroundings, this *avant-garde* actor and director uses stylized sets and conventionalized movements:

he gives us suggestion instead of reality, a symbol instead
of an imitation; and he relies, for his effects, on a new
system of lighting from above, not from below, and on a
quite new kind of drill, as I may call it, by which he uses
his characters as masses and patterns, teaching them to
move all together, with identical gestures. The eye is
carried right through or beyond these horizons of canvas,
and the imagination with it; instead of stopping entangled
among real stalks and painted gables.

Here, for once, we see the stage treated in the proper
spirit, as material for art, not as a collection of real objects, or the imitation of real objects.[44]

'In these remarkable experiments', he writes in another
article of the same year (1902), 'I seem to see the suggestion
of a new art of the stage, an art no longer realistic but conventional, no longer imitative but symbolical',[45] and he suggests that Craig's sets would be especially suitable for a
verse-play by Yeats.

The other aspect of Symons's 'symbolism', his hostility to
poetic grandiloquence, is expressed most clearly in *The
Symbolist Movement in Literature* in the essays on Verlaine
and Laforgue. Symons praises Verlaine for having liberated
French poetry from that 'rhetoric' which, because it seeks
above all to impress an audience, hinders the direct expression of the poet's emotions. In his essay on Laforgue, which
is in many ways surprisingly reminiscent of the impressionist
phase of his criticism, he praises Laforgue's 'subtle use of
colloquialism, slang, neologism, technical terms', and the
deliberate uncertainty of his rhythms. 'The old cadences, the
old eloquence, the ingenuous seriousness of poetry', he writes,
'are all banished, on a theory as self-denying as that which
permitted Degas to dispense with recognisable beauty in his
figures. Here, if ever, is modern verse, verse which dispenses
with so many of the privileges of poetry, for an ideal quite
of its own.'[46]

Similar attitudes recur in other essays of the period. Symons criticizes Oscar Wilde's *The Ballad of Reading Gaol* not only because of its didactic element, but because it 'has not entirely escaped "poetic diction" in its language'.[47] In his essay on Robert Bridges, whom he praises highly as a writer of 'purely lyric poetry', Symons agrees with him that poetry should follow the natural rhythms of speech, but objects to his use of inverted syntax. An inversion for the sake of a rhyme or rhythm, says Symons, is 'indeed an inexcusable blemish in a poem written frankly in the language of to-day. . . . It is a "poetic licence", and for poetic licences poetry, at all events modern poetry, has no room'.[48] Yeats is praised by Symons for his irregular, unemphatic rhythms, for his lack of syntactical inversions, and for his overall avoidance of grandiloquence. 'It is a common mistake', says Symons, 'to suppose that poetry should be ornate and prose simple.' On the contrary:

> It is prose that may often allow itself the relief of ornament; poetry, if it is to be of the finest quality, is bound to be simple, a mere breathing, in which individual words almost disappear into music. Probably to many people, accustomed to the artificiality which they mistake for poetical style, and to the sing-song which they mistake for poetical rhythm, Mr. Yeats' style, at its best, will seem a little bare, and his rhythm, at its best, a little uncertain. They will be astonished, perhaps not altogether pleased, at finding a poet who uses no inversions, who says in one line, as straightforward as prose, what most poets would dilute into a stanza, and who, in his music, replaces the aria by the recitative.[49]

Another variety of 'rhetoric' to be avoided, according to Symons, is the type of poetic imagery which is merely decorative. In Tennyson's 'Palace of Art', says Symons, 'the pictures and the statues are no more than decorations in a house of thought'.[50] An image by Landor, although it is both visual and scrupulously precise, is 'no more than . . . an ornamentation . . . to a thought separately clear in itself'. 'The image', complains Symons, 'is not itself the most vital part of the speech.'[51]

It is far from being the case that all poetic imagery is ornamental, however, as Symons makes clear in his essays on Yeats and Verhaeren, and especially in those on the critic Leslie Stephen and the Spanish poet Ramon de Campoamor. Leslie Stephen is quite right, says Symons, to claim that philosophy is 'in reality nothing but poetry expressed by the cumbrous methods of dialectical formulae', and he is equally right to claim that philosophy 'labours painfully to put together ostensible reasons for the truth of the conceptions of life which are directly presented in the poetic imagery'.[52] Symons agrees with Campoamor, too, that philosophical systems are no more than 'poems without images', and that poetry is 'the rhythmical representation of a thought through the medium of an image, expressed in a language which cannot be put in prose more naturally or with fewer words'.[53] For Symons, it seems, as for T. E. Hulme and Ezra Pound later, the image is in fact the staple of poetry. Poetic images, according to all three, can 'directly present' truths about reality which the discursive language of philosophy can only approximate to.

Much of what has been written above emphasizes themes which were always present in Symons's criticism. Before the final phase of his development is considered, it is important to take note of the significant innovations and changes of emphasis which distinguish his attitudes as a symbolist from his earlier attitudes as an impressionist. As we have seen, Symons had always advocated a form of poetry which could communicate the subjective experiences of the poet directly to the consciousness of the reader, and in this respect his criteria as a symbolist are no different from his criteria as an impressionist. What has changed is his view of the type of experience to be communicated. As an impressionist he had wished poetry to communicate the ephemeral moods and impressions of man in the modern city. As a symbolist he wishes poetry to communicate the 'sensations of the soul' in its experience of the divine. In the poetry of St John of the Cross, he writes in 1899, religious ecstasy strives to find the most direct form of expression, to find 'immediate, and no longer mediate, words for its revelation'.[54]

Symons's new religious seriousness brooks no didacticism in poetry, however. In 1897 he had praised Christina Rossetti because her devotional poetry is 'never didactic, or concerned with purposes of edification'.[55] In *The Symbolist Movement in Literature* he applauds Verlaine's ability to evoke pure emotion in the reader, untainted by moralizing or didactic comments: 'with Verlaine . . . the affection or the regret is everything; there is no room for meditation over destiny, or search for a problematical consolation'. Wordsworth, on the other hand, committed 'the heresy of instruction', as Symons remarked in 1902. Although right to believe that poetry can be a kind of religion, Wordsworth forgot that 'what is preached from the pulpit', or religious doctrine, is 'by no means of higher importance than what is sung or prayed before the altar',[56] or the direct communion of the soul with God.

We have seen that Symons had from his youngest days condemned the 'poetry of mere description'. In his essay of 1898, 'Ballet, Pantomime, and Poetic Drama', he describes the ballet as epitomizing the modern ideal in artistic expression because in the ballet 'Nothing is stated, there is no intrusion of words used for the irrelevant purpose of describing.'[57] In his essay on Laforgue in *The Symbolist Movement in Literature* he praises Laforgue for pursuing to its limit 'the theory which demands an instantaneous notation (Whistler, let us say) of the figure or landscape which one has been accustomed to define with such rigorous exactitude'.[58]

Whereas he had talked in his earliest criticism of 'flashing an image', however, Symons in this later phase talks in quasi-magical terms of 'evocation'. Mallarmé, he writes, attempts to 'evoke, by some elaborate, instantaneous magic of language, without the formality of an after all impossible description'.[59] The ballet-dancer who epitomizes the modern artistic ideal is 'all pure symbol', says Symons. She does not describe. Instead she 'evokes . . . idea, sensation, all that one need ever know of event'[60] by means of her beautiful movement alone.

The new, magical element in Symons's poetic is at its most evident in his comments upon Nerval, Mallarmé, Yeats and Verhaeren. Discussing Nerval and Mallarmé in *The Symbolist Movement in Literature,* he implies that poetry can communicate transcendental realities when its complex musical sound-pattern matches the network of occult correspondence which unifies all created things. By means of symbols, he says elsewhere, Yeats is able to express the divine and all-pervading ' "love which moves the sun and the other stars" ', the 'great secret' of which is whispered by all things in nature.[61] Somewhat differently, and possibly with Schopenhauer in mind, Symons says that in the poetry of Verhaeren symbols communicate 'primary ideas' from the spiritual world.[62]

While Symons continued, then, as he had done in 'The Decadent Movement in Literature', to encourage a 'revolt from the ready-made of language, from the bondage of traditional form', his view of the status of poetry had changed radically. In the introduction to *The Symbolist Movement in Literature,* epitomizing the symbolist movement as an attempt to spiritualize literature and to free it from the bondage of materialism, Symons warns that literature thus liberated incurs the highest responsibilities. It 'becomes itself a kind of religion, with all the duties and responsibilities of the sacred ritual'.

Having claimed for symbolist works what can only be the sacramental status of the Eucharist, Symons was clearly obliged to reject some formerly admired authors as unworthy, and to present others in a worthier light. As an impressionist he had greatly admired the brothers Goncourt. In *The Symbolist Movement in Literature* the brothers Goncourt are brusquely dismissed as scientific realists. Villiers de l'Isle-Adam, who had always figured in Symons's earlier criticism as the wickedly 'perverse' author of the *Contes Cruels,* has now become above all the visionary author of *Axël.* Verlaine, hitherto the urban-impressionist poet of the *Romances sans Paroles,* has now become a religious poet, the 'great poet of *Sagesse*'.

Revaluations of an increasingly radical kind were to force themselves upon Symons in the final stage of his criticism, as we shall see.

iv

Expressionism might be described as symbolism on the offensive. Like the symbolist movement of the late nineteenth century, this early-twentieth-century movement in the arts is to a considerable extent underwritten by mysticism, but generally of a vitalistic rather than a quietistic kind. In its tone and attitudes it owes much to the dynamic evolutionism of Nietzsche and Bergson. Like symbolism, and for much the same reasons as those just described in connection with Arthur Symons, expressionism strongly opposes realism and impressionism. It does so on the additional and thoroughly Romantic ground that these movements had degraded the unique figure of the creative artist into a merely servile instrument for producing what Symons called the 'mere imitation' of everyday reality. Far less withdrawn than the symbolists, the expressionists were very much more positive and aggressive in opposing *mimesis* and in proclaiming the powerfulness and uniqueness of the artist's creative and essentially visionary imagination. Admiration for 'energy' played a central part in the aesthetics of such expressionists as the Italian futurists and the English vorticists, and these two groups in particular were extremely hostile to the morbid and erotic elements which had characterized the visions of many so-called symbolist poets and painters in practice.

As Arthur Symons's views became considerably more vitalistic during the last phase of his criticism, and his way of presenting these views considerably more aggressive and polemical, I have taken the liberty of calling this phase 'expressionist', although he never to my knowledge used this term himself. After 1900 he increasingly demanded that works of art should possess the qualities of 'energy' and 'vision'. 'L'énergie', he came to agree with Baudelaire, 'c'est la grâce suprème.'[63] These changing criteria led him to dismiss most of his earlier heroes, while the tone of his criticism became increasingly violent, especially in his denunciation of 'the mob'.

As a champion of Browning, Symons from his earliest days as a critic had scolded those who look to poetry for 'the solace of an afternoon cigar'.[64] By 1896 his condescension to the middle classes had begun to turn into denunciation of the mob, and readers of *The Savoy* were reminded that 'Art . . . must always be an aristocracy.'[65] In 1898 he decisively rejected Tolstoy's argument that the greatest art appeals to the greatest number, declaring democracy to be impossible in the realms of art and intellect. 'There', he writes, 'at all events, we must always find an aristocracy; there, at all events, the stultifying dead-weight of equality must for ever be spared to us.'[66]

One of the most consistent implications of *The Symbolist Movement in Literature* is that the composition of the best literature is necessarily accompanied by an aristocratic disdain for the public. After the turn of the century, however, the tone in which these opinions are expressed becomes markedly less urbane. In 1903, for example, Symons writes about newspapers as follows:

> What royalties and religions have been, the newspaper is. . . . As well deny the power of folly, which is the voice of the mob; or of the mob, which is the mouth-piece of folly. The newspaper is the fulfilment of the prophecy: that the voice of the people shall be the voice of God. It is the perpetual affirmation of the new law which has

abolished all other laws: the law of the greatest wisdom
of the greatest number.

The newspaper is the plague, or black death, of the
modern world. It is an open sewer, running down each
side of the street, and displaying the foulness of every
day, day by day, morning and evening.[67]

This denunciation of the mob was accompanied by a quiet
but steady rejection of Symons's idols of the nineties, and
one might infer that Symons would have broken with his
critical past more openly if he had been in a financial position to forgo the republication of his earlier books and
articles in praise of these writers.

The brothers Goncourt had been dismissed in 1899, as
we have seen. In 1900 Degas was accused of ugliness, and
Whistler of triviality.[68] Materlinck was found guilty of
'rhetoric' in 1902.[69] The painters Henry de Groux, Félicien
Rops and Gustave Moreau, formerly admired as symbolist
visionaries, were written off in 1904 and 1905. Much more
surprisingly, the novelist Huysmans was written off with
them.[70] By 1907 even the work of Verlaine had been called
into question. In the second edition of *Plays Acting and
Music,* which was not actually published until 1909, Symons
amended his original article on 'Pachmann and the Piano'.
In his amended version he tells us that the delicate art of
Whistler and Verlaine, though preferable to the emphatic
art of Zola and Kipling, is nevertheless inferior to the great
art of Rodin and Wagner. In the work of Rodin and Wagner
'we have weight as well as sharpness'; he writes, 'these giants
fly'.[71]

Symons had first acclaimed violent emotion, energy, and
'divine excess' in his essay on Balzac, which had been published several months *before* he brought out *The Symbolist
Movement in Literature.* Balzac realized as the Greeks did,
he says, 'that human life is made up of elemental passions
and necessity', but the novelists who came after Balzac have
banished great emotions and 'primary passions' from the

novel. The 'probable novelists' of Symons's day, basing their characterizations upon 'nerves and a fatalistic heredity', have left scarcely any room in the novel for the 'dignity and disturbance of violent emotion', and their characters have come to resemble 'diaphanous jelly-fish, with balloon-like heads and the merest tufts of bodies'.[72]

In his essay of 1906 on Ibsen and in the second edition of *Plays Acting and Music* Symons writes similarly concerning drama. Great drama, he says, deals with the relationship of man's soul to the universe. Its characters are 'ultimate types of energy'[73] such as Lear, Oedipus, and the people of Wagner's operas, and the 'primary emotions' experienced by the souls of these superhuman figures can be expressed only in verse.

Energy and affirmation are the qualities for which he praises Blake and Nietzsche throughout his *William Blake* (1907). In Blake's poetry, he writes:

> there is no moral tendency, nothing that might not be poison as well as antidote; nothing indeed but the absolute affirmation of that energy which is eternal delight. He worshipped energy as the well-head or parent fire of life; and to him there was no evil, only a weakness, a negation of energy, the ignominy of wings that droop and are contented in the dust.
>
> And so, like Nietzsche, but with a deeper innocence, he finds himself 'beyond good and evil,' in a region where the soul is naked and its own master.[74]

The striking changes which had taken place in Symons's attitudes since he had written the quietistic conclusion to *The Symbolist Movement in Literature* are well summed up in his 'Hymn to Energy', a poem of four stanzas written in 1902. Just as God is the unwearyingly energetic artist of creation, he argues in this curiously didactic poem, so each of us should be 'artist of his [own] days'. The first stanza describes God in Neo-Platonist terms as the source from which all life and energy emanate:

God is; and because life omnipotent
Gives birth to life, or of itself must die,
The suicide of its own energy,
God, of his unconsuming element,
Remakes the world, and patiently renews
Sap in the grass and ardour in the wind,
Morning and evening dews,
And tireless light and the untiring mind.

Symons's position in the last stanza of this poem is the exact
opposite from that taken up at the end of *The Symbolist
Movement*. The reader is not encouraged to resign himself
to 'forces which it is our wisdom to obey'. On the contrary,
he is assured of his own God-like energy and instructed to
employ it as a means to self-transfiguration:

Thou art, as God is; and as God outflows,
Weaving his essence into forms of life,
And, out of some perfection's lovely strife,
Marries the rose's odour with the rose,
So must thou of thy heavenly human state,
And of thy formless strife and suffering,
Thyself thyself create
Into the image of a perfect thing.[75]

The changes which had taken place in Symons's personal
attitudes during the short space of eleven years are made
dramatically apparent when we compare 'Going to Hammersmith' with 'Hymn to Energy'. At a much more general level,
however, the latter poem might also be regarded as sympto-
matic of the way in which the introverted, unassertive and
sometimes precious aestheticism of the 1890s would change
into the extraverted, hard and aggressive aestheticism of the
'men of 1914'. Both the 'nineties men' and the men of 1914
are perhaps indebted ultimately to Walter Pater for the
conviction expressed by Symons in this poem, that life should
be converted into art. The difference between Wilde, say,
and the vorticists, is often one of tone rather than basic
doctrine, and it is in the new, self-confident and dynamic
tone which was to prove typical of the coming generation of

artists and men-of-letters that Symons has begun to speak in this poem.

In the light of these developments it seems likely that Symons's enthusiastic review of Joyce's *Chamber Music* (1907) is a conscious reversion to his own earlier manner, written to help a struggling young author at a time when he himself was committed far more to the energetic and visionary gospel of Blake and Nietzsche than to such 'tiny, evanescent things'[76] as Joyce's extremely ninetyish poems.

v

Symons's criticism is important and significant in two main ways. In the first place it reflects certain general trends of thought which appear central to the Age of Evolutionism. In the second place it contains a surprisingly large number of ideas about art and literature which anticipate those of the imagists and vorticists and which have subsequently won a great degree of acceptance. The serious literature of the first half of the twentieth century followed very closely the lines laid down by Symons: the theatre dispensed with realistic techniques, a related attempt was made to re-introduce poetic drama, the 'interior' novel predominated, and poetry was stripped of all that Symons deemed spuriously 'poetic'.

Like many of his contemporaries whose sense of the meaningfulness of life had been undermined by High Victorian scientism, Symons turned to occult doctrines in search of a unifying principle. His mysticism is 'a theory of life which . . . seems to harmonize those instincts which make for religion, passion, and art, freeing us at once of a great bondage'.[77] The key-note of his mysticism, as the last phrase reminds us, is one of optimism and liberation. This optimism, like Symons's élitism, is highly characteristic of the period 1880-1920. So too, it should be added, are his leanings towards scientific method in criticism. For despite his hostility to science, and despite the fluctuations in his critical opinions, he aspired apparently to formulate 'a theory, or system of aesthetics, of all the arts'. In the preface to the first edition of *Plays, Acting, and Music* (1903) he criticizes writers on aesthetics who confine themselves to the study of a single art-form, claiming that a 'universal science' of beauty is attainable. The diction of this note ('laws', 'theory', 'first principles', 'studies', 'science') is much more reminiscent of Herbert Spencer than of Walter Pater.

Equally characteristic of the period is the symbolist view of art and literature which was the aesthetic corollary of Symons's occultism. Furthermore, Symons's later criticism exemplifies the shift from symbolism to expressionism which took place in the early years of the twentieth century. His 'expressionist' phase and his rejection of the nineties antici-pate some of the important developments in the arts, epito-mized in the vorticist movement, which took place in London in the years immediately preceding the outbreak of war in 1914. Symons foreshadows something of this movement's polemical tone, its interest in violence, and its worship of 'energy'. He also anticipated its rejection of realistic 'imita-tion' in favour of expressionist abstraction. We have seen, for example, that he praised the 'new, abstract beauty' brought about by stylization and convention in the theatre. He similarly praised the drawings of Aubrey Beardsley, as Wyndham Lewis was to do in *BLAST*,[78] for their rejection of naturalism. Beardsley, he wrote in 1898, has been released 'from the bondage of what we call real things' by a sense of physical form 'so intense that it becomes abstract . . .'[79]

Symons was demonstrably a highly influential critic and translator. Yeats, in 'The Trembling of the Veil', acknow-ledges the importance of Symons's translations,[80] whilst Eliot has described how *The Symbolist Movement in Literature* introduced him in 1908 to the work of Laforgue, Verlaine and Rimbaud.[81] Ezra Pound, writing in 1911, listed Symons as one of his 'gods', together with Plato, Dante, Spinoza, Long-inus and Pater.[82] When Pound writes in 1914 that 'The gulf between evocation and description . . . is the un-bridgeable difference between genius and talent',[83] there seems little doubt that the distinction derives directly from Symons.

From about 1890 onwards Symons was the chief spokes-man in English for ideas concerning pure poetry which gradually ossified into that draconian legislation known as the modern or twentieth-century poetic. Throughout his career he strove to rid poetry of didacticism, moralizing and description, together with such forms of 'rhetoric' as poetic diction, inverted syntax, and decorative imagery. He was not of course the sole advocate of such views during the 1890s. Yeats makes this clear in *The Oxford Book of Modern Verse,* and Pound was well aware that 'The whole set of "The Rhymers" did valuable work in knocking bombast, & rhetoric and victorian syrup out of our verse.'[84] A. C. Bradley, in his 'Poetry for Poetry's Sake' (1901) argues for the autonomy of poetry and against poetic decoration.[85] Nevertheless, there is little doubt that Symons was the most insistent and force-ful advocate of such views in England during the 1890s, and it seems justifiable to infer a strong and direct influence upon his contemporaries and immediate successors.

As noted earlier, the remarks made by Symons, particularly during his earlier impressionist phase, often anticipate the theoretical pronouncements of the early-twentieth-century imagists. In his well-known 'Lecture on Modern Poetry' of 1914, for example, T. E. Hulme tells us that modern poetry 'has become definitely and finally introspective and deals with expression and communication of momentary phases in the poet's mind',[86] and that in this it resembles modern im-pressionist painting such as Whistler's.

Elsewhere Hulme tells us that 'Images in verse are not mere decoration, but the very essence of an intuitive lan-guage.'[87] It will be remembered that in his earliest criticism Arthur Symons had praised Browning, Meredith and the impressionists for their ability to flash a non-descriptive image directly to the consciousness of the reader. In his com-ments upon Leslie Stephen and Ramon de Campoamor, made during his symbolist phase, he anticipates the claims

of Hulme and Pound that poetical images express as precisely as possible what discursive prose can do no more than
inadequately paraphrase. His comments upon Landor's
imagery, moreover, anticipate almost to the letter the famous
distinction drawn by Pound between the meaningful imagery
of Cavalcanti's poetry and the merely ornamental imagery
of Petrarch's.[88]

Like Symons during his impressionist period, the imagists
encouraged verbal experiments whose aim was the truly
accurate communication of the poet's inner experience. They
chose 'To use the language of common speech. . . . To create
new rhythms—as the expression of new moods. . . . To allow
absolute freedom in the choice of subject.'[89] At a more fundamental level, Pound, Hulme and the imagists are in close
agreement with Symons about both the subject-matter of
poetry and its *modus operandi,* as I shall argue in my concluding chapter. Meanwhile it should already be apparent
that the modern movement in English poetry was very far
from being a simple and straightforward reaction on the part
of the modernists against their immediate predecessors. The
only significant novelty in imagist *theory,* for example, is its
advocacy of the free verse which Symons had rejected twenty
years previously.

4

Art for Evolution's Sake
Alfred Orage

Alfred James Orage, familiarly known as Alfred *Richard* Orage, was born on 22 January 1873, at Dacre in Yorkshire. When his father died soon afterwards, the widow and her four children returned to Fenstanton, the village in Huntingdonshire from which the family originated. The family was so poor that Orage could not have continued to attend the village school without the help of the local squire, who also helped him to attend a teachers training college at Abingdon, near Oxford, during 1892 and part of 1893.

In 1893 Orage went as an elementary-school teacher to Leeds, in Yorkshire. He had been converted to socialism during his time at college, and once in Leeds helped form a local branch of the newly founded Independent Labour Party. Between 1895 and 1897 he wrote a weekly 'Bookish Causerie' for Keir Hardie's weekly socialist magazine *The Labour Leader*. In 1896 he married, and in or about the same year joined the local branch of the Theosophical Society, of which he became a leading member. In 1900 he met the young Holbrook Jackson, who introduced him to the work of Nietzsche, and in the same year the two men joined forces with the architect Arthur J. Penty to form the lively and successful Leeds Art Club.

In 1905, having taught for twelve years in Leeds, Orage resigned from his position, left his wife, and went to London. Here he stayed for a time with Arthur Penty, who had preceded him to London, and tried to live by serious journalism. During 1906 and 1907 he published articles in *The Monthly*

Review, The Theosophical Review and *The Contemporary Review*. His first book, *Friedrich Nietzsche: The Dionysian Spirit of the Age,* was published in 1906. Two more books were published in 1907: *Nietzsche in Outline and Aphorism,* and *Consciousness: Animal, Human, and Superman.* The two works on Nietzsche were the first systematic introductions to Nietzsche's thought to be published in book form in England.

During these early years in London Orage also attempted to found a Gilds [*sic*] Restoration League with Arthur Penty. This venture failed, but Orage and Holbrook Jackson, who had also come to London, succeeded in founding a Fabian Arts Group. This group was intended as a rallying-ground for socialists who thought the arts of fundamental importance, and who were consequently opposed to the bureaucratic Fabian socialism of Sidney and Beatrice Webb and their supporters.

Early in 1907 Orage and Jackson bought an existing periodical called *The New Age* for £1,000, half of which was put up by George Bernard Shaw. Orage and Jackson became joint editors, but Jackson resigned after a few months as a result of disagreement over policy. Under Orage's editorship *The New Age* quickly established itself as a leading journal of political, literary and artistic debate. Established writers such as Wells and Shaw contributed free of charge, and articles by the English Nietzscheans (J. M. Kennedy, A. M. Ludovici and Oscar Levy) appeared regularly. Always eager to encourage new talent, Orage was the first editor to publish work by Richard Aldington, F. S. Flint, Katherine Mansfield, Edwin Muir and Middleton Murry. According to one of his letters Ezra Pound owed his life to Orage's financial support.[1] Orage was also the first editor to publish the work of T. E. Hulme, and between 1912 and 1914 *The New Age* regularly reproduced cubist and vorticist paintings and drawings.

The New Age was always a journal of discussion and debate, in whose pages Orage himself often disputed with his own editorial staff. In the first three years of his editorship its policy appears to have been mainly that of providing a forum in which the many varieties of current socialist opinion could be expressed. After 1910, however, in a period of rapidly mounting social and political violence, *The New Age* became increasingly a vehicle for political and literary neo-feudalist views of the kind described in Chapter 1, and in 1912 it began to advocate guild-socialist policies editorially.

Although the outbreak of war in 1914 rendered the guild socialist movement virtually irrelevant, a National Guilds League was formed in April 1915, and *The New Age* continued as the official organ of the movement until this foundered through internal dissension in 1920. For some time before this happened, however, Orage's own interests had been turning in other directions. He had become increasingly involved in the Social Credit policies of Major C. H. Douglas, the mystical doctrines of P. D. Ouspensky, and the psychoanalytical doctrines of Freud. These changes of direction in Orage's thinking after the 1914-18 war are reflected in the changed subtitle of *The New Age*. Previously 'A Weekly Review of Politics, Literature, and Art', it became in January 1921 'A Socialist Review of Religion, Science, and Art'.

In 1922 the mystical teacher G. I. Gurdjieff arrived in London, and plans were made to found the Institute for the Harmonious Development of Man at Fontainebleau-Avon in France. In October 1922 Orage resigned from *The New Age* in order to join Gurdjieff at the Institute. In December of the following year he went to New York to lecture on the aims of the Institute, remaining in the United States in this capacity until 1930. During this period he published a series of retrospective articles entitled 'An Editor's Progress' in *The New Age* for 1926, and two collections of his earlier weekly literary articles for *The New Age: Readers and Writers* (1922) and *The Art of Reading* (1930). His own contributions to *The New Age* between 1907 and 1922 had been as follows: 'Towards Socialism' (ten articles in 1907); the mainly political 'Notes of the Week' between 1909 and

1922; 'Unedited Opinions' (a series of eighty-six Platonic dialogues, between 1909 and 1916); seven anti-feminist 'Tales for Men Only' (1911, 1912, 1916); 'Readers and Writers', a weekly article of literary reviews and comment which appeared between 1913 and 1921.

Orage returned to England in 1930, but did not resume editorship of *The New Age*. He decided to found a new periodical during the financial crisis of 1931, and *The New English Weekly* began publication in April 1932 as the organ of the Social Credit movement. Orage died in November 1934, and was succeeded as editor of *The New English Weekly* by Philip Mairet, his subsequent biographer. Among the many admiring letters on Orage published in the obituary number of *The New English Weekly* of 15 November 1934 was one by T. S. Eliot, who described him as being, during his editorship of *The New Age,* 'the best literary critic of that time in London'.

Orage's *Selected Essays and Critical Writings* were edited by Herbert Read and Denis Saurat and published posthumously in 1935. His *Political and Economic Writings* were edited by Montgomery Butchart and others, including T. S. Eliot, and published in the following year. His translation of Gurdjieff's *Meetings with Remarkable Men* was not published until 1962.

ii

Socialism in the 1890s was no merely economic plan for the State-ownership of the means of production. As Orage described it in 1926 it was 'much more of a cult, with affiliations in directions now quite disowned—with theosophy, arts and crafts, vegetarianism, the "simple life," and almost . . . with the musical glasses. Morris had shed a mediaeval glamor over it with his stained-glass News from Nowhere. Edward Carpenter had put it into sandals . . .'[2]

Of these various affiliations and influences, the two most obvious in Orage's own early writings for *The Labour Leader* are those of the arts and crafts movement, and of Theosophy.

As a follower of William Morris (and, behind Morris, of Carlyle and Ruskin), Orage holds the Liberal creed of commercial competition responsible for the decadence and disintegration of contemporary art and society. As a Theosophist he looks to spiritual evolution as a means of restoring wholeness to art and to social life.

Orage's unremitting campaign against social and literary decadence began in *The Labour Leader* in 1895, which was the year of Nordau's *Degeneration* and the Wilde trial. Reviewing a new American literary magazine entitled *Moods*, he writes as follows: 'America needs . . . a physician. It is down with the "yellow fever." The English "Yellow Book" has got cured just too late to stop the spread of the infection, and America has now its "Moods." The usual symptoms appear, things Weirdsley wonderful, impressionism, and weakness.'[3] This decadence has not been brought about by the degenerate nature of individual artists, however, but by commercial competition:

> I do not believe in the absolute decadence and degenerateness of modern times. . . . But it is . . . only too obvious that the 'damnable commercialism which buys and sells all things' is sliming our literature and lowering for a while our standard of art. This degradation . . . is the natural outcome of the same spirit manifested in our system of economy, in science, in politics, and in life.[4]

It is commercial competition, according to Orage, which has caused some modern writers to go 'hopelessly astray . . . in the pursuit of mere commercial success', and as a consequence 'The high traditions of literature have fallen into the hands of men who betray them for thirty pieces of silver.' Although much modern literature is 'mere literary pathology, analysing, dissecting, diagnosing disease', this is the fault of the commercial system, which is itself 'an unnatural life which has brought about the conditions which our novelists describe'.[5] Commercialism has also corrupted the standards of criticism, complains Orage in his obituary article on William Morris:

> Our system of competition, based on the degradation of the vast majority of mankind, has won us baubles which we fondly believe to be pearls of great price, but at the cost of works of priceless value, the best that human souls might do, in art, literature, craftsmanship, life, for whose loss no future age can forgive us, and for whose loss it is our shame that we can still forgive ourselves.[6]

In attacking a society based exclusively upon commercial competitiveness Orage reveals the direct influence of Morris. Elsewhere in his articles for *The Labour Leader* he reveals the Theosophical 'affiliations' of his socialism, making it clear that the sources of his guiding beliefs in Theosophy and evolution are mainly literary. Among those whom he describes as having helped to familiarize Western students with 'the "divine science" of the East' are not only Max Müller, Schopenhauer and the Theosophists, but Sir Edwin Arnold, Rudyard Kipling, the authoress Flora Steel, and, especially, Walt Whitman and Edward Carpenter.[7]

The basis of Orage's Theosophy is his belief in the concept of the universal self or world-soul, which he was to describe in 1907 as 'a perfectly similar underlying consciousness common to all living things, visible and invisible'. Orage was converted to this doctrine of the universal self by reading Edward Carpenter's *Towards Democracy* and Walt Whitman's *Leaves of Grass,* and it was Whitman who also confirmed his belief in mankind's evolutionary progress towards god-head. Whitman, says Orage, 'taught us plainly what the oldest Rig Vedas had mistily written, . . . that God himself is perfect man, and the goal of every speck of dust'.[8]

The critical applications of Orage's evolutionary mysticism are best seen in his two articles for *The Labour Leader* on Edward Carpenter's *Towards Democracy*. In the first of these he defends Carpenter's use of free verse on the grounds that it embodies the rhythms of the life which pervades the universe, and that it consequently enables the poet of democracy to integrate men more closely into the universal self to which he and they belong:

> to knit men closer with themselves and nature by expressing nature in man; to electrify and vitalise the dormant nerves which connect the heart of Nature with her outlying limbs; to express the universal in terms of humanity—this is the function of the poet of Democracy.[9]

It may not be immediately apparent that Orage is here proposing a social function for poetry: poetry creates social wholeness, knitting closer together men who have been disunified and set against each other by 'our system of competition'.

Although poetry has this extremely important function, Orage is reluctant to discuss the kind of meaning that it possesses. In his second article on Carpenter he defines poetry as 'the expression in words of the universal in man' and poetic rhythms as 'the embodiment in words of the movement of life'. These definitions are probably less important than the grounds upon which Orage justifies them. 'It will be said that these are vague phrases . . .', he comments. 'Vagueness, however, is inevitable from the very nature of great poetry; but it is the vagueness of [trying to discuss] the illimitable.'[10] As will be seen in the next section of the present chapter, these views did not change when, after 1900, the thought of Nietzsche was added to the already diverse list of influences upon Orage's socialism. Great art was always to remain for Orage 'an expression of the illimitable', and though he was always a fervent advocate of great works of literature, holding them to be of the highest social importance, he was always reluctant to discuss their meaning in any detail.

Before his Nietzschean phase is discussed, it is worth remarking that the views put forward in 1896 by this twenty-three-year-old elementary-school teacher in his articles on Edward Carpenter, and published in an obscure socialist weekly, have certain basic similarities to those expressed some three years later by Arthur Symons in *The Symbolist Movement in Literature*. Orage's universal self is another name for the universal consciousness which Symons puts forward as 'the central secret of the mystics' in *The Symbolist Movement*. For both men, literature of the proper kind serves as a unifying force. 'What is Symbolism', asks Symons, 'if not an establishing of the links which hold the world together?'[11] For both men it is the *sounds* of poetry which achieve this unification by embodying the occult universal life which permeates all created things. As Orage puts it:

> if poetry is to express the 'Universal Idea', it must embody the 'Universal Idea': that is, it must be the counterpart in words of the universal in essence.
>   . . . that rhythm most nearly approaches perfection which most nearly corresponds to the rhythm of life. Colour, form, and sound—all of which words may suggest—have their place also; and generally speaking the more perfect the form of poetry the more perfect its embodiment of the rhythm, colour, form, and sound of life.[12]

The difference between prose and poetry, according to Orage in the latter of these two articles, is that 'prose must have something to say, while poetry has only something to express'. Prose makes statements *about* life, in other words, while poetry embodies and expresses the universal life force itself.

iii

In the third section of this chapter I discuss the ideas expressed by Orage in a number of books and articles published between 1902 and 1907, when he was responding enthusiastically to the doctrines of Nietzsche. I examine in turn Orage's highly evolutionistic views upon three inter-related topics: the coming of what Galton had called a 'highly gifted race of men', the place of this race in the socialist State of

the future, and the rôle of the arts in furthering the development of this new society.

According to Holbrook Jackson it was a momentous occasion when he introduced Orage to the work of Nietzsche in
the year 1900: 'did we not on that occasion build a bridge
from the Orient to the Occident? You left behind you . . . a
translation of the *Bhagavad Gita;* and you carried under
your arm my copy of the first English version of *Thus spake
Zarathustra.*'[13]

The occasion is a revealing one. It reveals of course that
intelligent young Englishmen at the turn of the century were
keenly interested in Indian mysticism and the thought of
Nietzsche. The occasion is more neatly symbolic than at first
appears, however, for the bridge was built from orient to
occident and not in the reverse direction. Orage, like a number of his contemporaries, did not by any means abandon
his existing beliefs under the influence of Nietzsche. Instead
he adapted Nietzsche's views to a predominantly Theosophical view of things, presenting him as a mystic who was no
longer consciously in sympathy with his own mysticism. No-
one who really understands Nietzsche, he tells us, 'will doubt
that behind all his apparent materialism there was a
thoroughly mystical view of the world'.[14] On one occasion
he even went so far as to describe Nietzsche's doctrine of the
will-to-power as 'perhaps the nearest Western approach to
the intellectual formulation of *one* of the aspects of the
mystical Trinity'.[15] Just as J. M. Kennedy saw Nietzsche as
a second Benjamin Disraeli, so Orage (in company with
Arthur Symons[16] and W. B. Yeats[17]) saw him as a second
William Blake. '. . . he who has read *The Marriage of Heaven
and Hell,* and grasped its significance', writes Orage, 'will
have little to learn from the apostle of *Zarathustra.*'[18]

Similarly, Nietzsche's gospel of the superman was grafted
by Orage onto notions of man's high evolutionary destiny
which he had already derived from a variety of sources. His
first mention of Nietzsche is in fact contained in an article
on Lytton's *Zanoni* in *The Theosophical Review* for 1902.

Here he approves of the desire of Mejnour, Zanoni's fellow magus, to create a 'mighty and numerous race' of superhuman occult adepts, even if this necessitates the sacrifice of thousands of aspirants for the sake of a single success. 'Such an ideal', writes Orage, 'can be paralleled perhaps in the work of a real man . . . Frederic Nietzsche; and the parallel is almost complete when one finds Mejnour saying of himself, "my art is to make man above mankind".'[19]

The superiority of the Nietzschean superman is not of course physical. 'Nowhere is Nietzsche to be taken less grossly than in his conception of power', writes Orage in his *Nietzsche in Outline* (1907). 'The men of power in his eyes are not the men of sinew and brawn, but men in whom the power of mastery over both themselves and others is greatest.'[20] Nor is the superman 'merely man writ large', he writes in his *Friedrich Nietzsche* (1906). 'It is probable . . . that new faculties, new modes of consciousness, will be needed, as the mystics have always declared; and that the differencing element of man and Superman will be the possession of these.'[21]

In his *Consciousness: Animal, Human, and Superman* (1907) he suggests that 'superman consciousness' will in fact be a continuous state of visionary ecstasy. In the course of evolution, animal consciousness has become 'folded' upon itself and produced human self-consciousness. A second evolutionary folding will by analogy produce the *ecstasis* of superconsciousness:

> superman, or . . . cosmic consciousness, is consciousness in three dimensions, or human consciousness folded upon itself. . . . the typical product of [this] folding is to create another observer appearing to stand outside the human mind, as the human observer appears to stand outside the animal mind. If analogy is any guide, we may . . . say that the dominant characteristic of the superman state in relation to the human state is a standing outside, or ecstasis.[22]

In short, Orage's superman will be a mystic who has attained to a permanent condition of 'cosmic consciousness'. On balance he appears to owe less to Nietzsche than to the race of superhuman mystical adepts foreshadowed earlier for English readers by Bulwer Lytton and Madame Blavatsky.

Like his books on Nietzsche and superman consciousness, Orage's articles of 1906-07 on education, politics, and the arts and crafts movement are primarily devoted to the fostering of a new race of men of genius, to the encouragement of 'the few alone who give new significances to things'. In his two articles on education ('Esprit de Corps in Elementary Schools' and 'Discipline in Elementary Schools') he criticizes the 'appalling uniformity of schools and teachers' in State schools. In his article entitled 'Politics for Craftsmen' he condemns the English socialist parties for their drift towards policies of State collectivism. All three articles strongly oppose standardization and social levelling, and call for measures to increase individualism. 'The hope of Europe lies in its great individuals', according to Orage, and they alone can check what he calls 'the devastations of democracy'.[23]

The socialist movement as a whole, he claims in 'Politics for Craftsmen', has betrayed 'the interests of artists, craftsmen and imaginative minds generally' by concentrating all its efforts on improving the economic conditions of the working class. He protests against this 'exclusive association of Socialism, which in its large sense is no less than the will to create a new order of society, with the partial and class-prejudiced ideals of the working man'.[24]

The inspiration of socialism is nothing less than the creation of a new civilization, states Orage in his series of articles entitled 'Towards Socialism', which appeared in *The New Age* during 1907. The improvement of purely economic conditions is no more than a preliminary to the accomplishment of this utopian task: 'Abolish poverty for us, and our men of genius will then begin their cyclopean task of building a civilisation worthy of the conquerors of titans.'[25] Great individuals are necessary to the creation of this new socialist civilization because men are led forward by such 'noble illusions' as religion, nationalism, beauty, honour and glory. These illusions are usually formed for them by the small number of men of creative imagination upon whom a civilization ultimately rests. 'Civilisation', says Orage, 'is no more than the possession by a people of individuals . . . capable of inspiring great enthusiasms, and of individuals . . . capable of being so inspired. The rest is all but leather and prunella.'[26]

In an article of 1907 entitled 'The New Romanticism', Orage equates these great individuals with the 'guardians', the élite class of Plato's ideal republic. Life is intolerable, he states, without some illusion to pursue, and the function of legislators is to provide the majority with a viable illusion. 'The question for legislators (I have Plato's guardians in my eye, Horatio) is which of the possible illusions is at once most necessary, most beneficent, and most enduring.'[27] Whether or not these great individuals were to constitute a definite aristocratic caste is a matter upon which Orage equivocates. In 'Politics for Craftsmen' he rebukes the Labour Party for having no interest in a 'reconstructed society arranged in some such hierarchy of human values as Plato sketched and Mr. Wells has lately revived.' (The reference is to Wells's *A Modern Utopia*, which is governed by an aristocratic caste of so-called Samurai.) In 'Esprit de Corps in Elementary Schools' Orage proposes 'that almost forbidden word aristocracy' as his possible alternative to the uniform and egalitarian society aimed at by the collectivists. 'Call it if you will', he says '. . . the Hierarchy. The idea at least is the same, namely the classification of children, schools, institutions, yes, the whole State, in the ancient Platonic way of iron and brass and silver and gold.'[28]

In 'Towards Socialism' Orage appears to reverse these views, however, claiming that contemporary advocates of a new aristocracy have been misled. Mankind basically prefers 'all the horrors of freedom to the amenities of benevolent slavery', he says. 'Hence not only a hereditary aristocracy is ridiculous, inhuman, and in the long run impossible, but an aristocracy of intellect, character, or what not, as well.'[29] He makes it clear however that his ideal socialist state of the future is to be led by an evolutionary élite of noble minds. Socialism will provide increasing opportunities for the development of great creative individuals. These will command the service of the majority not by coercion, however, but by the beauty of their visionary ideas, and Orage looks forward to a 'State in which personal desire is poured out like wine in offering to the great lords of life'.[30]

That the 'great lords of life' come from *Zanoni* rather than *Zarathustra* is a point of minor interest. The major interest of Orage's élitism is twofold: it is entirely characteristic of the period 1880-1920 that evolution should be thought of as producing a new breed of men of genius, or great individuals, and it is equally characteristic that these new evolutionary notions should be used in support of proposals which were far from new, such as 'the ancient Platonic way'.

In his articles on Edward Carpenter's *Towards Democracy* Orage had claimed that poetry such as Carpenter's served a social purpose: that of bringing men closer together in socialist brotherhood. Nietzsche provided him with a quite different concept of the way in which literature might help in the creation of a new socialist civilisation, and one of the guiding principles of his criticism after he had absorbed the influence of Nietzsche may fairly be expressed in the phrase 'art for evolution's sake'. While Nietzsche modified Orage's views on the *function* of art, as will be seen, he did not however modify Orage's views on the *content* of art in the least. 'Nietzsche's main view emerges clearly enough in this form', he writes in his *Nietzsche in Outline*. ' "Ecstasy as both cause and effect of all great Art." '[31]

This belief that art communicates the indefinable *ecstasis* of the visionary artist continues to be central to all Orage's affirmative criticism. In 1902, for example, reviewing Arthur Machen's *Hieroglyphics,* he agrees with Machen that 'All great art is symbolic'. Art is not concerned with the everyday world, he says, but with the spiritual world by which we are surrounded. Only the mystic knows where art and literature originate, 'for his whole life lies in the world whence literature and art have come—the world that begins where the world enclosed by the five senses ends'. It is the duty of Theosophists, whom Orage has chided for their neglect of the arts, to work for the revival of a literature which expresses these transcendental realities:

> far from having nothing to say to the literary man the Theosophist has everything to say; . . . no less than the rejuvenation of religion, is his work the restoration of its ancient lights to literature, that literature may become, as once it was, the handmaid of the Spirit sacramental in its nature, and divinely illumining for the darkling sight of men.[32]

The view of art presented in Orage's *Consciousness* is equally other-worldly. According to this book, art is one of the chief means by which an evolving mankind is made aware of its 'marvellous powers to come'. Like religion, love, nature and great men it is 'a perpetual reminder of the reality and . . . the possibility of the continuous ecstatic state', lifting us 'out of our duality into a sphere where for an instant we become one of Plato's spectators of time and existence', and in which we are 'above our human mode of consciousness, freed and released, superconscious'.[33]

As far as the *function* of art is concerned, the most important chapter in Orage's two books on Nietzsche is that on 'Willing, Valuing and Creating' in his *Nietzsche in Outline*. Here he emphasizes that artists and philosophers are uniquely important in the evolutionary process of 'becoming' which constitutes the sole *raison d'être* of the universe, for they alone are capable of creating the new imaginative values which will inspire mankind to create the superman. According to Orage's paraphrase of Nietzsche, the world as we perceive it is entirely 'an imaginative creation, the work of great creative and imaginative artists who . . . brooded upon the face of shapeless and meaningless chaos'.[34] Artists, that is, provide mankind with meaningful interpretations of the human situation, and in doing so create ideals: 'where the artist leads there the people follow; he is the standard-bearer, the inspiring pioneer, the creator of new worlds, new values, new meanings . . .' It follows from this that art cannot be an end in itself. It has a moral value, although its morality is not that of any specific or transient moral code:

> In the sense that Art is thus the great stimulus to life, the enchanter who unfolds or creates alluring vistas, and so seduces the will to the task of the eternal becoming, Art is moral. But the morality is not that of any creed or Sinaitic tablets or transient mode of life, but of life itself. Art for Art's sake means in effect, says Nietzsche, no more than 'Devil take morality.'[35]

In the past, to continue Orage's paraphrase, the philosopher's rôle has been to test the new values created by the artist, on behalf of the human race as a whole. In the future, however, their rôles will be reversed. It is the philosopher who will create the new ends and meanings which will lead mankind towards the superman, while the artist's rôle will be to make these attractive, to 'glorify and englamour them'.

Given the concept of the superman as the goal of human progress, states Orage in his *Friedrich Nietzsche,* 'it becomes possible to estimate the values of things in specific terms'. For Orage himself it now appeared possible to judge art and ideas in terms of their evolutionary value. Far from being an incidental to human life, art was crucially important in a double sense, for by rendering attractive things which were inimical to the evolutionary process the artist might subvert life instead of enhancing it: 'Because . . . Art is the great seducer to life it may also be the great seducer to death . . . and the artist may be saviour or traitor to the race.' Orage readily accepted the Nietzschean view that 'All art . . . is either ascendant or decadent, either leads the will upwards to increase and power, or downwards to decrease and feebleness.'[36] Decadent art is that which works against evolutionary progress towards the superman, in other words, and ascendant art is whatever encourages it. Or, as Orage put it in *The New Age* during 1920, 'The test of literature is whether it gives and intensifies life or takes away and diminishes life.'[37]

One cannot complain that Orage does not think sufficiently highly of the arts, nor would one wish to quarrel with the view that works of literature, for example, can provide us with new interpretations and evaluations of human experience. As we have seen, Orage talks of the 'new ends and meanings' which philosophers are to create and artists are to make attractive. His visionary concept of great art made him always reluctant to discuss these ends and meanings in any detail, however. In his criticism for *The New Age,* to which I now turn, he continued to maintain that the meaning of great literature could not be discussed on an everyday level, stating for example that poetry is 'mystical, super-rational',[38] and that 'Drama begins where reason leaves off.'[39]

iv

The fourth and fifth sections of this chapter are devoted to the increasingly polemical criticism published by Orage in *The New Age* after 1910. In the present section I discuss his attacks upon social anarchy and literary realism between 1910 and 1912, and in the section which follows I discuss his weekly articles entitled 'Readers and Writers', which began to appear in 1913.

There is a marked change in Orage's attitudes and tone from late 1910 onwards, whether he is discussing politics, feminism or literature. In his articles of 1907 entitled 'Towards Socialism' he had taunted the cautious and bureaucratically minded Fabian socialists by declaring that every good socialist was a utopian. His attitudes only four years later were very different. The only remaining Conservatives, he wrote in 1911, 'are a handful of Tories . . . and a few Socialists like ourselves. All the rest have joined in the wild goose chase after "social reform", "progress", "democracy", or some equally chimerical fowl.'[40]

The increasing conservatism of Orage's attitudes and the increasingly violent tone in which he expressed them are probably best understood in the light of the major social upheavals which were taking place at the time. 'As the summer of 1914 opened', writes Paul Johnson, 'Britain was on the verge of civil war . . .'[41] The years 1910 and 1911 in Great Britain introduced a period of social anarchy which, but for the outbreak of war, would have culminated in the projected general strike of 1914. The spread of syndicalist doctrines caused an unprecedented number of industrial strikes during 1911, and a general strike was threatened for August of that year. The battle for women's suffrage intensified in violence after the riots of Black Friday (18 November 1910), while the constitutional crisis of 1911 concerning the House of Lords was followed by equally desperate political struggles over the Irish Home Rule Bill and Lloyd George's National Insurance Bill. The latter was regarded by many, including Orage and Hilaire Belloc, as an ominous move in the direction of a collectivist 'servile State'.

Orage's opinions on the suffragette movement provide a good index of his increasingly conservative attitudes during these years. In one of his 'Unedited Opinions' of 1909 entitled 'Votes for Women' he had spoken approvingly of female emancipation. In 1912, however, he attacked the movement as one of feminine self-contempt, declaring in the following year that the female revolt could occur only because 'the instincts have lost their unity and become anarchic'.[42]

During 1911 and 1912 Orage also published in *The New Age* six 'Tales for Men Only', moral fables which describe in great psychological detail the disastrous effects of female influence upon the masculine creative imagination. The

structure of all six tales is basically the same, the narrator
R. H. Congreve (Orage's usual pen-name) being *primus
inter pares* of a group of artist-philosophers who are 'intent
on creating between them a collective soul or superman'.
In their evolutionary attempt to 'form a communal mind,
which . . . shall constitute a new order of being in the hierarchy of intelligent creation',[43] they have found women to
be their greatest obstacle. In the second of these tales, for
example, the poet Freestone is warned that his poetry will
inevitably deteriorate if he continues to rank his girl-friend
higher than his poetic muse: 'From mythopoeia you will
descend to symbolism, and if that is too obscure for the girl,
down you will go to valentines.'[44]

The fourth of these tales stands out from the rest by reason
of its greater satirical liveliness. Its protagonist, the political
scientist Tremayne, is guilty of 'the last infirmity of noble
minds . . . the ambition to cure a woman of femininity'. He
unsuccessfully attempts to educate a Mrs Foisacre, a woman
whose furnishings are as 'promiscuous' as her mind and
morals:

> Her room was quaintly furnished, for all the world as if
> relays of minor poets had each been given a cubic yard
> to decorate. On this wall were the deposits of the French
> Symbolist school—drawings of spooks and of male and
> female figures shaped like vegetables. On that wall were
> photographic reproductions of the Parthenon friezes; the
> high-water mark, I suspected, of some pseudo-classic youth
> who yearned to be strong. The floor was covered with
> matting, and an earthenware fountain in the midst played
> by means of a pump. There was a piano and a host of
> divans. Oh, divans, I thought. Divans! What a lollipop
> life we are in for! Turkish delight, scented cigarettes,
> lotus-land, minor poetry, spooks—and where is the guitar?
> There, as I live, hanging behind the door![45]

Mrs Foisacre is also described as an embodiment of 'Maya'
(the world of illusory appearances) and 'the mob'. She is

clearly and revealingly intended by Orage as a complex em-
blem of contemporary social anarchy, sexual promiscuity,
cultural disunity, and artistic decadence.

There is an equally strong change of emphasis in Orage's
comments upon literature after 1910. In 1909 he had confidently announced that 'We are now standing . . . at the
cradle of a second English Renaissance in Art, Literature,
and the Drama.'[46] In his 'Unedited Opinions' of 1910 he
began a series of violent attacks upon the realistic novelists
of the day for 'poisoning' their readers. He was not alone in
voicing criticism of this kind, however, for a number of
critics were complaining at this time of the 'sordid' and
'blasphemous' elements in the works of such authors as John
Galsworthy, John Masefield, Eden Philpotts, Laurence
Housman, and Lascelles Abercrombie. In 1912, for example,
in *The Nineteenth Century and After,* the well-known English positivist Frederic Harrison attacked what he called
'The Cult of the Foul' in contemporary literature,[47] while
Degeneration itself rose from the depths again in April 1913
after an interval of fifteen years.

In his own strong opposition to realism, as in his belief
that 'all great art is symbolic', Orage is extremely close to
the Arthur Symons who wrote *The Symbolist Movement in
Literature.* He is equally close to Oscar Wilde, who in 'The
Decay of Lying' (1891) had earlier distinguished between
the 'imaginative reality' of Balzac and the 'unimaginative
realism' of Zola, describing Zola's realism as 'the true decadence . . . from [which] we are now suffering'.[48] When Orage
attacks realism as the product of commercialism, and rejects
certain literary topics on aesthetic rather than moral grounds,
he displays the influence of William Morris. Where he differs
from such 'nineties men' as Wilde, Morris and the earlier
Symons, and what characterizes him as a 'man of 1914', is
above all the violence of his tone.

Orage announces the general grounds of his opposition to
realism in his dialogue on 'Modern Novels' (1910). He also
reveals in passing two sources of his belief in neo-feudalism

and occult supermen (Disraeli and Lytton respectively). Contemporary realistic novelists are so severely criticized by his reviewers for *The New Age,* he says, because they poison their readers with commonplace representations of reality. Instead of doing this, they should provide their readers with a stimulus to the noble life. 'Disraeli and Lytton are in my opinion the two English novelists who aimed highest', writes Orage, 'though I admit they fell far short in actual achievement. Their heroic characters were at least planned on the grand scale.'[49]

So strong is Orage's concern for correct evolutionary development that he will not allow literary artists to describe ugly and sordid aspects of life in order to condemn them, for even this is to run the risk of making vice attractive: 'To add to the poison-fangs of the snake its glittering fascinating eye is . . . to give it strength', he claims.[50] Nor will he even allow art to acquaint us with the worst aspects of life in order that we may face them more courageously. The purpose of art is not to involve itself with the concerns of everyday life at all, he writes, but to promote spiritual progress: 'Progress in the spiritual meaning is . . . a perpetual running away from what is generally called life. . . . How mistaken to define as the purpose of art the very contrary of the purpose of the most spiritual! Yet such as declare that art is for the purpose of bracing us for life obviously do this.'[51]

In these *New Age* dialogues, as in his earliest articles for *The Labour Leader,* Orage relates realism in literature to commercialism in society. The great artist, he claims in 'Money-Changers in Literature', cannot give of his best in an atmosphere poisoned by commercially minded authors who 'teach the world to measure success by circulation, to regard literature as a commodity to be advertised and boomed like pills, to despise poor artists as living out of touch with their times, to attach to literature the meretricious adjuncts of contemporary gossip, social utility, fashionable crazes, topical discussions . . .'[52]

It is consequently the duty of critics, who 'cannot be too severe', to reveal the destruction caused by these commercial authors or 'usurping demagogues'. Critics must first expose the second-rate artists who deal in pain and brutality, the nine out of ten modern artists who 'do nothing but glorify mad-houses, lock-hospitals and ugly accidents'.[53] But they must also be severe with certain genuine and dedicated artists who mistakenly believe that the subject-matter of works of art should be free from restrictions. 'With our modern ideas of liberty, universality and democracy', writes Orage, 'it is difficult for artists to remember that these ideas are not for them. They resent . . . the limitations which former artists deliberately put upon themselves; with the consequence that the most uncouth materials are to be found in modern works.' Orage criticizes the 'uncouth materials' to be found in realistic novels, not on moral grounds, but on aesthetic grounds. Against the view that it is only the literary treatment of a subject that matters, he argues that certain types of subject-matter can never be made beautiful:

> . . . I should say that disease ought never to be treated by the artist; likewise vulgar murders, rapes, adulteries, kitchen squabbles, the doings and sayings of vulgar and repellent persons, the sexual affairs of nonentities, the trivial, the base, the sordid, the mean. . . . The rejection is not primarily on moral grounds, but on aesthetic grounds. These things simply cannot be made beautiful. . . . The literary artist should no more employ his pen on them than a painter would put mud and rubbish on his palette.[54]

Orage presents his moral critique of realism as an aesthetic critique because of his reluctance to allow that literature communicates *ideas* in the everyday sense of the word, a reluctance particularly evident in his strictures upon realism in the contemporary drama. He condemns as 'mummery' the type of play in which ideas are discussed, and dismisses the notion of propagandist art as a contradiction in terms. 'The

sole object of a work of art', he argues, 'is to reveal beauty
and to leave that beauty to affect whom it may. Surely, it
argues a small belief in beauty if we must add to it a moral
or a purpose other than itself. . . . It is in the nature of all
spiritual things that they are above utility.'[55] Writing in
1912 he describes genuine drama as being, like all genuine
art, 'sacramental', a claim which is virtually identical with
that made for symbolist works by Arthur Symons. According
to Orage true drama is a 'pentecostal art', a religious cere-
mony which concerns and addresses man's immortal soul,
and which like the Mass conveys an experience which cannot be communicated in words:

> Actions that we can rationalise, explain, forecast, deter-
> mine, are actions motivated in the reasoning brain. With
> them drama has nothing to do, for drama is the repre-
> sentation of a mystery. . . . Drama begins where reason
> leaves off. . . . Drama is the representation and therewith
> the illumination of the subconscious. We are made to
> *feel* that we understand, though we are aware that our
> understanding cannot be expressed in words. Deep calleth
> unto deep.[56]

That our understanding of great literature cannot be expressed in words is a position which Orage continued to
maintain in his 'Readers and Writers' articles of 1913-21,
to which I now turn. In these articles he continues the
polemical critique of contemporary social and literary decadence which he had begun in 1910, frequently undertaking
to demonstrate the decadence of contemporary literature by
making what would now be called a 'practical criticism' of
chosen extracts. He continues to be reluctant to discuss
great works of literature in any detail, however. Their greatness is apparently subject to no such demonstration as applies
in the case of decadent writing, and we must consequently
rely upon Orage's assertion that certain works are supremely
great. Orage's statements that the highest poetry is 'in the
octave beyond the rational mind',[57] and that in Milton's

prose 'The sense is nothing, but the supersense is every-thing',[58] remain consistent with his earliest claims that great poetry communicates 'the illimitable' and can therefore be discussed only in the most general terms.

v

Orage resumed his criticism of contemporary literature and society in his weekly 'Readers and Writers' column, which began in *The New Age* in 1913 and continued until 1921. Extremely polemical at first, the tone of his criticism became less so after 1915, by which time the entire social and literary situation had been changed by the Great War.

Instead of discussing general issues as he had done in his dialogues of 1910-12, Orage intended in this column to dis-cuss the particular events of each week, consistently, seriously, and with definite ends in view. In other words, his literary criticism was intended as an integral part of a much wider programme, the aim of which was to create a unified and orderly guild-socialist commonwealth in place of a society rendered in his view increasingly anarchic by the divisive Liberal creed of unrestricted commercial competition. Be-cause weekly literary events follow no obvious pattern, as Orage later conceded, his hopes for this column were not entirely fulfilled. Nevertheless, in its strategy and its critical attitudes it possesses a consistency which is far from apparent in such published selections from it as *Readers and Writers* and *The Art of Reading*. Removed from the context of *The New Age*, moreover, its significance as part of a programme of cultural reform is also entirely lost.

As we would expect, much of Orage's criticism in 'Readers and Writers' is directed against the commercialization of literature. He regularly indicts such manifestations of com-mercialism as the best-sellers of H. G. Wells and Arnold Bennett, the 'booming' of books by publishers, the critical irresponsibility of such literary journals as *The English Re-view* (at that time under the editorship of Austin Harrison), and the type of journalistic reviewing, such as that of the *Daily News,* which can describe a trilogy of novels by Oliver Onions as 'the highest sustained product of English literary creative genius in the present century'.[59]

Decadence continues to be another of Orage's favourite targets. Concerning that ninetyish magazine *The Gypsy,* for example, he writes: 'The association of art with luxury, of beauty with disease, of aesthetic emotion with strange and sought sensations, is the unholy union of god and ape that we have set ourselves to annul.'[60] By 'decadence' however he means much more than the eroticism of the 1890s. He claims that decadence in literature exemplifies the decadence and anarchy (and for Orage the terms are virtually inter-changeable) of the entire age. Concerning a proposed study of the poet John Davidson by Frank Harris he writes, for example: 'A study of such a congeries of moods unhappily gathered in a single consciousness must be a diagnosis more of our times than of a man; and its name should not be Davidson but Anarchism.'[61]

On similar grounds he attacks a variety of allegedly inter-related targets: contemporary realist authors, for example, and such contemporary exponents of 'infantilism' and 'deca-dence' as the imagists, vorticists and futurists. He suggests that a connection exists between 'Imagism and Savagery, be-tween anarchic verse and anarchic conduct, between Mr. Pound's images and Mr. Wyndham Lewis' "Blast." '[62] Of Pro-fessor Gilbert Murray he writes that his mind is 'eclectic, that is to say, it lacks unity, is anarchically tolerant of incon-gruities'.[63] Ezra Pound's prose-style he describes as 'a pastiche of colloquy, slang, journalism and pedantry. Of culture in Nietzsche's sense of the word—a unity of style—it bears no sign'.[64] Of G. K. Chesterton and the age as a whole he writes: '. . . Mr. Chesterton, though a critic of our days, is its most complete incarnation; all styles are to be found in him save any style; all ideas save any idea; all points of view save any point of view'.[65] Examples need not be multiplied. It appears highly likely that in mounting his attack upon contemporary social and literary decadence in 'Readers and Writers' Orage made fuller use of what I have earlier called Bourget's formula than any other English cultural critic before or since.

In this column he continues to attack the commercially inspired book-reviewing of the day and frequently calls for severer standards of criticism. Describing contemporary critics as the worst ever known in any period of literature, he insists that it is the business of the critic to make judgements, and that these should be moralistic in intent. 'I can imagine no critic worth his office', he writes, 'who does not judge with a single eye to the upholding of the moral laws. Far from being an offence to literature, this attitude of the true critic does literature honour. It assumes that literature affects life for better or worse.'[66]

Orage's own judgements in 'Readers and Writers' are uncompromisingly harsh, and their unusual freedom of expression brought *The New Age,* as he commented later, into 'somewhat lively disrepute'.[67] They rest, however, on two basic assumptions: that literature should have (*a*) an evolutionary function, and (*b*) a visionary content.

As he expresses it in 'Readers and Writers', Orage's view of the proper function of literature is that it should further evolutionary progress. The writer's duty is to lead men forward by creating noble illusions to which they will aspire. 'If poets and imaginative writers want subjects for poetry', he agrees with the French socialist philosopher Proudhon, 'let them make it out of the visions of what humanity may and ought to become.'[68] The business of the artist, he states elsewhere, is to 'forward Nature by divining her plans and manifesting what is in her mind'.[69] An evolutionistic view of the function of literature also underlies his Wildean distinction between realism of a Zolaesque kind and that 'true' or 'imaginative' realism which foretells what Nature will or might produce in the future, and thereby 'raises literature to a great art again'. In 'Readers and Writers' Orage praises writers so unalike as Longinus, Sorel, and (time and again) the author of the great Hindu epic the *Mahabharata,* because these authors have in common the qualities of nobility and sublimity which are essential to evolutionary progress.

Orage's undeviating insistence that the proper content of literature is visionary is seen at its clearest in a statement, reprinted in his *Selected Essays and Critical Writings,* in which he concludes that art has 'nothing to do either with emotions or with ideas'. Art, he goes on to say:

> arises from the creative contemplation of the artist and arouses in the beholders a corresponding appreciative contemplation. Both artist and critic are on the super-conscious plane: the one creating symbols for its expression and the other experiencing its life in contemplation. All art thus plunges the beholder into a high state of reverie or wonder or contemplation or meditation; and that is both its nature and its purpose. We should suspect a work professing to be art when it arouses either [emotion] or thought. Unless it can still both of these inferior states, and arouse us to contemplation, it is human, all too human.[70]

This distrust of 'thought' in art and literature leads Orage to claim in 'Readers and Writers' that the 'quasi-magical effect of certain forms of literature is independent of the ostensible content', so that in Milton's prose 'It is not what he says that matters in the least, but it is the style in which he says it. The sense is nothing, but the supersense is everything.'[71] Elsewhere Orage distinguishes between the 'common sense or matter' of literature and the 'super-sense of words, or style'.[72]

In 'Readers and Writers' Orage often undertakes a practical criticism or detailed critical analysis of particular passages. These probably represent an effort to secure for his judgements something of the prestige attaching to the scientific method, and he does on one occasion claim that 'we ought to be able to apply a scientific stylometry to literature in general'.[73] The questionable and Bourget-like assumption behind Orage's critical analyses, however, is that an author's moral decadence is evident in the decadence of his literary style. Although Havelock Ellis had urged his readers to recognize that 'decadence is an aesthetic and not a moral conception', Orage claims to be able to perceive moral decadence 'in the very construction of a man's sentences, in his rhythm, in his syntax'.[74] In fact, whether he is analysing Meredith or the military critic of *The Times,* he devotes nearly all his attention to the rhythm of the passage which he has selected, and scarcely any to its paraphrasable meaning. He always prefers to say, not that an author's thinking is illogical or that his ideas or attitudes are morally unacceptable, but (with Bourget and Nietzsche) that his *style* is decadent. Orage's stylistic analyses thus allow him to pass moralistic judgements upon an author's work whilst ignoring the morality of the views which the work itself advances.

In his unwillingness to discuss the meaning of even a poor piece of literature Orage is being entirely consistent with his views on the nature of art as we have seen them expressed above. His other-worldly concept of art renders him extremely reluctant to concede that the meaning of any work of art, good or bad, can be adequately discussed. 'It is not without reason', says Arthur Symons in *The Symbolist Movement in Literature,* 'that we cannot analyse a perfect lyric.'[75] Here, as in a number of important respects, Orage is at one with him, claiming that the more great literature is analysed, 'the more mysteriously beautiful it becomes'.[76] I return to this and allied topics in my final chapter after making my concluding remarks upon Orage.

vi

Orage might be considered as a type-figure of the critic in the Age of Evolutionism. Evolutionistic assumptions play a dominant part in all his thinking, whether he is advocating that society be led by a new breed of men of genius or attacking literary decadence because it is contrary to desirable evolutionary tendencies. He is equally typical in using these evolutionistic assumptions as a means of restating thoroughly traditional ideas. His guild socialism is firmly rooted in the neo-mediaeval tradition of Pugin, Disraeli and Morris. Furthermore, as noted in Chapter 1, he believes that evolution is proceeding to the golden age *backwards*: 'To go back is to go forward', he writes in 1915. '. . . the rediscovery of ancient Indian culture will give us the Europe of to-morrow. Nothing else will.'[77]

He is also a characteristic figure of the period 1880-1920 in his belief in Theosophy and mysticism, those movements which, as we also saw in Chapter 1, replaced for many serious-minded people a Christian world-view apparently discredited by biblical criticism and by High Victorian scientism. Orage's visionary aesthetic, which is an important corollary of his mysticism, is also characteristic of the period. So too is his use of the prestige of science itself in carrying out his 'stylometric' critical analyses. Although I have not discussed the developing interest in psychoanalysis which is apparent in 'Readers and Writers', it appears characteristic of Orage and a number of his contemporaries that this new and would-be scientific development should have been quickly incorporated into a programme for achieving superconsciousness.

Orage's criticism also importantly exemplifies that shift in tone, noted in Chapter 1 and already mentioned in connection with the final phase of Arthur Symons's criticism, which appears to be an important element in the shift from symbolism to expressionism. A basic hostility to realism links Orage to Yeats and the later Symons on the one hand, and on the other hand to such *avant-garde* modernists of the next generation as Pound, Lewis and Hulme. This hostility to realism also links him to Oscar Wilde, in whose 'The Soul of Man under Socialism' and 'The Decay of Lying' are to be found a significant number of notions which Orage was later to express far more polemically. Although he decisively rejected what he called the 'yellow fever' of the nineties, Orage continued to respect Wilde for his Nietzschean view that nature imitates art, just as the vorticists continued to respect the implicit anti-realism of Pater's theories[78] and of Beardsley's practice.[79] Orage himself appears to have been instrumental in re-stating the aestheticism and the symbolism of the nineties in the new hard and assertive language of early-twentieth-century expressionism.

As John Holloway has pointed out, Orage's attack upon the commercial debasement of literature and of literary criticism anticipates attitudes which were later taken up in *The Calendar of Modern Letters* and *Scrutiny*.[80] Orage's detailed critical analyses of particular passages, to which he regarded biographical and historical information as irrelevant, anticipate in certain important respects the subsequent approach to literature of I. A. Richards and the New Critics. As an important platform for classicist and neo-feudalist views concerning literature and politics, *The New Age* from about 1910 onwards anticipates much that was to appear later in the thought of Wyndham Lewis and T. S. Eliot.

The New Age was not by any means, of course, solely a platform for views of this kind. Although Orage himself was committed to guild socialism as an editor, as a political commentator, and as a literary critic, *The New Age* was above all an arena for controversy and debate. In his rôle of severe and intolerant critic Orage fiercely condemned both futurism and imagism. In his rôle of tolerant and broad-minded editor, on the other hand, he was one of the first to publish the work of both futurist painters and imagist poets. He constantly sought and encouraged new talent; as a result of his editorial catholicity *The New Age* continues to merit our attention and admiration as without doubt the most intellectually alive and seminal periodical of its day.

5

A *Kind* of *Religion*

I wish to suggest finally and in particular that early-twentieth-century modernism is indebted to the occult revival and the symbolist aesthetics of the period 1880-1920 to such an extent that it cannot be properly understood without reference to them. There are formidable difficulties in the way of meaningful generalization here, such as the many shifting senses of the terms 'occultism', 'symbolism' and 'modernism' themselves, the enormous variety of literary and artistic practice during the past fifty or sixty years, and the fact that certain important modern authors such as D. H. Lawrence and Ernest Hemingway appear to have had no connection whatsoever with either occult doctrines or symbolist theories of the transcendental kind. Nevertheless, I believe it can be shown that doctrines and theories of this kind have powerfully affected such major twentieth-century writers as T. S. Eliot, James Joyce, Ezra Pound and Wyndham Lewis, that they continue as a strong undercurrent in contemporary literary criticism, and that while they have radically upgraded the status of art and artists in twentieth-century society, they continue to have a limiting effect upon contemporary poets and painters, who are by this time probably unaware of the ideological origins of their own practice.

What I have called the Age of Evolutionism ended during the Great War of 1914-18, taking its millennial optimism and most of its evolutionary assumptions with it. Most of us nowadays will probably hold it as an assumption that mankind has evolved from some earlier species. We believe this, in other words, probably without knowing or caring much about the evidence for our belief. Unless we are Marxists or followers of Teilhard de Chardin, however, we will presumably not subscribe either consciously or unconsciously to any other of the articles of evolutionary faith which were so much taken for granted during the period 1880-1920. As I hope to have shown in this study, an awareness of the extent to which the period was dominated by evolutionary assumptions seems necessary if we are to come to terms with its literature and literary criticism.

To understand all is not necessarily to forgive all. We shall better understand what now appears to be the proto-fascism of an Orage or a Hulme, however, when we realize the extent to which it was underwritten by the evolutionary élitism of scientists like Galton. Similarly, we shall better understand Kipling's talk of 'lesser breeds', however distasteful this may now appear, when we have read the chapter entitled 'The Comparative Worth of Different Races' in Galton's *Hereditary Genius*. We shall better understand, also, the late-nineteenth-century and early-twentieth-century revival of occultism, which in its own right has not always been kindly dealt with by mid-century critics. In his volume on modern writers in *The Oxford History of English Literature,* for example, J. I. M. Stewart describes it as an 'infection'. Concerning the interest of Yeats and his circle in astrology, Theosophy, and automatic writing, he writes as follows: 'If we remain surprised by the credence which he extended to so much seemingly ramshackle supernatural communication, we may reflect that it was a strong infection of the age.'[1]

There are good reasons, though, as we have seen, why such movements as spiritualism and Theosophy proved so contagious. Spiritualism seemed to offer the possibility of a scientifically demonstrable religious faith which would be capable of replacing or substantiating an apparently tottering Christian orthodoxy, and in England the movement was supported by such highly respected scholars as Henry Sidgwick and Sir Oliver Lodge. The Theosophical movement, more importantly, used the all-conquering concept of evolution as a spring-board by means of which such ancient transcendental doctrines as Brahmanism and Neo-Platonism might be re-asserted. Seen as an attempt to restore to men's experience of the world a harmony and a significance denied by such widely read materialist philosophers as David Strauss, Ernst Heinrich Haeckel and Ludwig Büchner (1824-99), the occultist revival as a whole seems perfectly comprehensible. It is also perfectly defensible, should one wish to take sides in these matters, for there is after all nothing remotely scientific about the determinism and materialist-monism of such philosophers as I have mentioned.

Each of the three figures discussed in detail in this book was deeply affected by the revival of occult doctrines which took place during the period which began in 1880. Ellis, Orage and the later Symons are all three, in their different ways, mystics, and all three might be described, in their different ways, as symbolists of the transcendental kind. According to Orage, the most uncompromising symbolist of the three, art expresses 'the super-conscious plane' by means of symbols, and has nothing to do with either human thought or human emotion. Symons, in *The Symbolist Movement in Literature,* makes clear that he is using the word 'symbol' in a transcendental sense by referring the reader in his introduction to the famous definition given by Carlyle in *Sartor Resartus*: 'In the Symbol . . . there is ever . . . some embodiment of the Infinite.' In his later criticism Symons implies that symbolist literature reveals the infinite in two ways, either by expressing through its rhythms the system of occult correspondences which articulates the universe, or by conveying 'primary ideas'. He also describes as symbolist the type of poetry which communicates the 'sensations of the soul' in its experience of the infinite. Havelock Ellis, too, claims that art embodies 'visions of the infinite'. The work of art, he says in the conclusion to *The New Spirit,* is able to convey directly to the soul of the beholder an 'external' (i.e.

transcendental) world of spiritual reality which philosophy can convey only discursively:

> The secret of the charm of art is that it presents to us an external world which is manifestly of like nature with the soul. . . . The work of art—poem, statue, music— succeeds in being what every philosophy attempts to be. . . . A Gothic cathedral of the thirteenth century is an embodiment of the infinite world itself.[2]

The views of all three critics have much in common with those of Schopenhauer, whose idealist aesthetic was briefly described in my first chapter, and they may in fact reflect his influence either directly or through some such intermediary as Walter Pater. According to Schopenhauer music is the highest art-form because it alone is capable of conveying ideas or supernatural realities directly to the soul of the auditor. Both Schopenhauer and Pater regard music as the highest art-form because it cannot be analysed, and both claim that the other arts approach perfection the more they approximate to the condition of music. Havelock Ellis follows exactly in Schopenhauer's footsteps when he writes in *The New Spirit* that music has the power to convey the profoundest and consequently least definable spiritual realities: 'In music', he says, 'the most indefinite and profound mysteries of the soul are revealed.'[3]

Ellis, Orage and the later Symons all resemble Schopenhauer in assuming that music and the verbal and plastic arts all convey or are trying to convey the same supernatural subject-matter, and that they therefore constitute 'art', which is a special mode of communication with the spiritual world. Ellis and Orage in particular habitually talk about art in the abstract, rarely distinguishing between the various individual art-forms, and still less rarely between the various genres of literature.

Neither Symons nor Orage will ever allow that genuine literature makes paraphrasable statements *about* human experience. Both consider that the attempt to analyse a perfect poem, for example, can reveal only an unanalysable and mysterious beauty, and incline to the view that its meaning resides less in its overt and paraphrasable content than in its rhythms and sound-patterns: in other words, presumably, that the 'music' of poetry conveys otherwise incommunicable spiritual realities to the soul of the reader. In the finest poetry, according to Symons, the meanings of words are secondary to their sounds: 'individual words almost disappear into music'.

Havelock Ellis, unlike Symons and Orage, is vitally interested in the statements which authors make about human experience. In order to justify discussion of these statements he is obliged, revealingly, to distinguish between two types of literature: the literature of art and the literature of life. The greatest literature, in his view, is 'all art'. Like the highest forms of art, which according to him are music and design, it is non-representational, and its meaning is consequently not open to discussion. 'In its chief but rarer aspect', writes Ellis in the preface to *Affirmations,* 'literature is the medium of art, and as such can raise no ethical problems. . . . Of the literature that is all art we need not even speak, unless by chance we too approach it as artists, trying to grasp it by imaginative insight.'[4] There is however a second type of literature which is not 'all art' and whose meaning can therefore be discussed and morally evaluated:

> But there is another kind of literature, a literature which is not all art—the literature of life. Literature differs from design or music by being closer to life, . . . only rising at intervals into the region of art. It is so close to life that largely it comes before us much as the actual facts of life come before us. So that while we were best silent about the literature of art, . . . we cannot question too keenly the literature of life. In this book I deal with questions of life as they are expressed in literature, or as they are suggested by literature. Throughout I am discussing morality as revealed or disguised by literature.[5]

In making this distinction between the pure literature of art and the impure literature of life, Ellis was able to escape, as Symons and Orage were not, from the *impasse* which is created when, with Schopenhauer and Pater, we categorize literature as art and postulate music as the condition to which all art should aspire. Of the three critics under discussion, Ellis alone was finally willing to allow in theory that the content of *some* literature might be descriptive of everyday reality, and that this content might be talked about and morally evaluated.

Turning from Ellis, Symons and Orage to early-twentieth-century creative writers, we find that Yeats is by no means the only one of these to have based his work upon some kind of occult doctrine. Wyndham Lewis, like Orage and the later Symons, certainly regarded the artist as necessarily a visionary:

> The production of a work of art is, I believe, strictly the work of a visionary. Indeed, this seems so evident that it scarcely needs pointing out. Shakespeare, writing his *King Lear,* was evidently in some sort of trance; for the production of such a work of art an entranced condition seems as essential as it was for Blake when he conversed with the Man who Built the Pyramids. . . . If you say that creative art is a spell, a talisman, an incantation— that it is *magic,* in short, there, too, I believe you would be correctly describing it. That the artist uses and manipulates a supernatural power seems very likely.[6]

There appear to be occultist elements in both the vorticism and the imagism of Wyndham Lewis's colleague Ezra Pound. Pound's vorticism as represented in his collection of essays *Gaudier-Brzeska* is heavily indebted to a work by one of Madame Blavatsky's many disciples: the well-known pioneer abstract painter Wassily Kandinsky, whose *On the Spiritual in Art* was translated into English by M. T. H. Sadler in 1914. On two occasions Pound refers in support of his vorticist principles to the *Holy Guide* by John Heydon,[7] the seventeenth-century Rosicrucian, and it may well be that his elusive and fundamental 'doctrine of the Image' is derived from the same author's *The Temple of Wisdome* (1664). Here is what Heydon has to say about 'telesmatical images', or images which have been endowed with occult powers:

> For they say, as the workers of the images do affect the image it self, so doth it bring the like passions upon those to whom it was ascribed, as the mind of the operator hath dictated it.[8]

Heydon's talismanic images work exactly as Pound's poetical images are supposed to, being in the nature of receiver-transmitters which cause the beholder (or reader) to experience the passions (or emotions) of the operator (or poet).

James Joyce's use of occult doctrines is given considerable prominence by Stuart Gilbert in the third chapter of his pioneering survey of *Ulysses*. Discussing Joyce's use of concepts such as metempsychosis, Karma, *manvantara* and *pralaya,* and of the doctrine of hermetic correspondences or universal analogies, Gilbert quotes such sources as Eliphas Lévi, A. P. Sinnett's *Growth of the Soul* and *Esoteric Buddhism,* Madame Blavatsky's *Isis Unveiled,* and Arnould's *Les Croyances Fondamentales du Bouddhisme.* 'It is impossible', he claims, 'to grasp the meaning of *Ulysses,* its symbolism and the significance of its leitmotifs without an understanding of the esoteric theories which underlie the work.'[9] When M. J. C. Hodgart concludes from his study of *Ulysses* and *Finnegans Wake* that Joyce 'considered occultism a suitable framework for his most serious literary conceptions, as Yeats did',[10] the claim seems in no way exaggerated.

T. S. Eliot's poetry, with its frequent references to occult doctrines and practices, and especially to Indian religious philosophy, similarly reflects certain dominant interests of the period 1880-1920. It is clear that Indian religious philosophy, and especially the asceticism which derives from it, were important and permanent influences upon Eliot's thought. This enduring interest, evident in Eliot's study of Sanskrit at Harvard University as early as the years 1911-13, is overtly reflected not only in his major work but in such minor poems as 'Burbank with a Baedeker; Bleistein with a Cigar', with its reference to the Buddhist 'seven laws'.[11] As Eliot's own notes to 'The Waste Land' indicate, the 'collocation of eastern and western asceticism' is central to this major poem, which refers its readers to the *Upanishads* as well as to the *Buddha's Fire Sermon*. A similar collocation is to be found in 'The Dry Salvages', where the references in the third section to Krishna and Arjuna, from the *Bhagavad-Gita,* are immediately followed and complemented by the prayer to the Virgin Mary which constitutes the fourth section.

An occult cosmology appears to be implied by several references in Eliot's work: 'the circuit of the shuddering Bear' in 'Gerontion', 'Gloomy Orion and the Dog' in 'Sweeney Among the Nightingales', and the 'perpetual revolution of configured stars' in *The Rock*. The second section of 'Burnt Norton' contains a brief passage of pure occult doctrine in which an occult correspondence is postulated between the structure of the human body and the structure of the universe:

> The dance along the artery
> The circulation of the lymph
> Are figured in the drift of stars . . .[12]

There are also several references in Eliot's work to divinatory practices associated with occultism. There are occult sibyls in both 'The Waste Land' and 'Gerontion' (Madame Sosostris and Madame de Tornquist), while Madame Blavatsky herself appears in 'A Cooking Egg'. Both 'The Waste Land' and 'Sweeney Agonistes' contain references to divination by means of playing-cards. While condemning such practices, the following well-known passage from 'The Dry Salvages' nevertheless reveals what is apparently a considerable expertise in matters of this kind:

> To communicate with Mars, converse with spirits,
> To report the behaviour of the sea monster,
> Describe the horoscope, haruspicate or scry,
> Observe disease in signatures, evoke
> Biography from the wrinkles of the palm
> And tragedy from fingers; release omens
> By sortilege, or tea leaves, riddle the inevitable
> With playing cards, fiddle with pentagrams
> Or barbituric acids, or dissect
> The recurrent image into pre-conscious terrors—
> To explore the womb, or tomb, or dreams; all these
>   are usual
> Pastimes and drugs, and features of the press:
> And always will be, some of them especially
> When there is distress of nations and perplexity
> Whether on the shores of Asia, or in the Edgware Road.[13]

It is arguable that both 'The Waste Land' and *Ulysses* are based upon different versions of the occult doctrine of correspondences between the human and divine worlds, and that they employ this doctrine in a similar vein of dramatic irony to suggest that the apparently random and pointless events of twentieth-century life are in fact part of the cosmic and spiritual pattern which unifies all creative things. Such a pattern may be implied in 'The Waste Land' by Eliot's use of the Tarot pack of cards, and in *Ulysses* by Joyce's use of Swedenborg's concept of the 'Grand Man'.

According to Swedenborg, all things on earth have their counterpart in heaven, which itself has human shape and is known to the angels as the Grand Man or Divine Man; each organ of our earthly human bodies corresponds to an organ of this heavenly Grand Man. Joyce himself was perfectly familiar with these notions, as may be seen from his lecture of 1912 on William Blake, which refers with evident approval to two of the most familiar of occult doctrines, the

notion of divine life flowing through all creation, and the
notion of correspondences:

> Eternity . . . appeared to the Swedish mystic [i.e. Sweden-
> borg] in the likeness of a heavenly man, animated in all
> his limbs by a fluid angelic life that forever leaves and
> re-enters, systole and diastole of love and wisdom. From
> this vision he developed that immense system of what
> he called correspondences which runs through his master-
> piece *Arcana Coelestia* . . .[14]

As each of the individual sections of *Ulysses* corresponds to
an organ of the human body the novel *in toto* may be seen
as constituting that supernatural human figure which was
Swedenborg's image for universal love and harmony, and
which Bloom and the other characters are unaware that they
are members of.

According to occult tradition during the period 1880-1920
the Tarot pack is nothing less than the legendary Book of
Hermes Trismegistus, and its individual cards are consequently the symbolic keys to all hermetic correspondences
between the human and divine worlds. I have pointed out
elsewhere[15] that 'The Waste Land' contains many more
references and allusions to these cards than Eliot acknow-
ledges in the notes to his poem, and suggested that he was
familiar with two books by A. E. Waite which present the
Tarot as a repository of hermetic doctrine: *The Pictorial
Key to the Tarot* (1911) and *The Hidden Church of the
Holy Graal* (1909). My general conclusion is that Eliot, by
building into his poem a system of correspondences based
upon the symbols of the Tarot, may have meant to imply
that his characters, though unaware of it themselves, were
taking part in a pre-ordained cycle of death and renewal at
a transcendental level. This earlier inference, made before
I was able to study the first versions of 'The Waste Land'
closely, has since been strikingly reinforced by an explanatory
passage which was deleted from the original drafts by Ezra
Pound as 'balls' (i.e. authorial, descriptive, discursive and

moralistic). Describing the people of London in familiar Buddhistic terms as 'bound upon the wheel' of earthly illusion, Eliot states that certain estranged minds, by which he presumably means his own, can see through to the 'ideal' or transcendental meaning of these apparently pointless twentieth-century lives:

> London, the swarming creatures that you breed
> . . . .
> Vibrate unconscious to their chords of destiny;
> . . . .
> Some brains, unbalanced from the natural equipoise
> (London! your people is bound upon the wheel!)
> Record the movements of these huddled toys
> And trace the painful, ideal meanings which they spell . . .[16]

A later conclusion to this passage, also deleted, implies that the highly imperfect world of everyday London is nevertheless a 'cryptogram' of the transcendental City of God.[17]

Like the writers just discussed, important early-twentieth-century artists in other fields were strongly influenced by occult doctrines: the abstract painters Kandinsky and Mondrian, for example, and the musical composers Holst and Scriabin. Gustav Holst, whose belief in astrology underlies his well-known suite *The Planets,* was like T. S. Eliot sufficiently interested in Indian mysticism to learn Sanskrit. Scriabin's *Poem of Ecstasy* recounts in musical terms the evolution of the human soul towards *ecstasis* or 'cosmic consciousness', a theme which dominates Orage's criticism and which is also expressed pictorially in Mondrian's *Evolution* triptych of 1911.

Both Kandinsky and Mondrian were Theosophists, and the underlying theory of the abstract painting which they pioneered and which has dominated European and American *avant-garde* painting until very recently, is that such works constitute a means of direct communication with the occult world. As Sixten Ringbom has so ably demonstrated, twentieth-century abstract painting is particularly and deeply indebted to the volume of *Thought-Forms* published in 1901 by the leading Theosophists Annie Besant and C. W. Leadbeater.[18] Martin S. James has convincingly summed up the aims of Mondrian and other early abstractionists as follows:

> Mondrian's Theosophy was more than a personal quirk. Several artists around 1910 sought through it deeper and more universal values, meanings behind meaning, new dimensions to understanding. The thought that ancient seers perceived and imparted a veiled wisdom, that behind the many guises of truth there is *one* truth, is partly based on Oriental and Neoplatonic ideas; it easily links with the Romantic and Symbolist theory of Illuminism (cf. Rimbaud's *Illuminations*), which gives the artist extraordinary, even occult power of insight into the nature of the world, the reality behind appearances—a new content for art.[19]

Their origins in late-nineteenth-century occultism all but forgotten, symbolist theories of literature appear to have continued to play an important part in twentieth-century literary criticism, and this during the identical period which has witnessed the establishment and spectacular rise of English literature as a field of study in schools and universities. On the one hand, as Frank Kermode has pointed out,[20] there has been a reaction in some quarters against certain major poets of the past, such as Spenser, Milton and Jonson; primarily, one supposes, because these poets committed what Arthur Symons called 'the heresy of instruction'. On the other hand, there has been an admiration in certain quarters for those works of literature which are most ambiguous and least capable of paraphrase. This admiration has its parallel and perhaps its origin in the view of such critics as Ellis, Symons and Orage that the finest works of literature are beyond discussion and analysis. Certainly those critics would have approved of both the notion and the quasi-theological overtones of Cleanth Brooks's term 'the heresy of paraphrase'.[21]

There are other ways, too, in which twentieth-century critical practice appears to be indebted to symbolist ideas of the period 1880-1920. A great many poems have been subjected to the process of practical criticism in learned books and journals, but many of these analyses pay much more attention to the sounds of the poem discussed than to its sense. So much so, that we might be justified in inferring that the authors of these analyses take the view, like Symons and Orage, that the kind of meaning poetry has, is conveyed through its sound-patterns. Again, numbers of critics appear to assume with Symons and his successors that the meaningful 'life' of a poem, novel or play resides almost solely in its imagery. In the field of prose-fiction, other critics devote their attention not so much to the words on the page as to the fundamental archetype or myth which the novel or story allegedly embodies, and which allegedly speaks to the reader's psyche at a level deeper than that of the rational mind. This might be regarded as a way of re-introducing Schopenhauer's supernatural 'ideas' in a form which is no more than ostensibly secularized.

I wish to suggest, in conclusion, that the aesthetic proposed by the symbolists of the period 1880-1920 has played an important part in shaping subsequent Western attitudes towards literature and the arts, and that it has considerably restricted the range of subsequent poetry and painting in particular.

The essential and most far-reaching symbolist claim is that art is 'a kind of religion', and the artist by definition an occult initiate: a kind of priest, visionary or magus who has privileged access to the transcendental world. I think it is fair to say that during the twentieth century this ultra-Romantic quasi-religious view of the status of art and artists has gained considerable ground in Western societies among both public and artists alike. The art of the past and present has been treated with increased reverence by the educated public, and the rôle of artist played with increased *hauteur*. At the same time the occult component of the symbolist aesthetic has encouraged artists to disclaim understanding of their own work and to leave the reader or spectator to make of it what he will. These distant and unaccommodating attitudes have alienated important modern writers and artists from an increasing section of the general public, thereby contributing to and accentuating the marked twentieth-century split between 'highbrow' and 'lowbrow' art and literature.

Such a split would scarcely have been conceivable by such High Victorian writers as Dickens and Tennyson, who wrote for the general public and were concerned to make themselves comprehensible to it. Where Dickens and Tennyson wrote about matters of public interest and concern, furthermore, twentieth-century art and literature have been to a large extent private, withdrawn and subjective. The subject-matter of the arts has shifted from the public to the private, and this appears to be a consequence of the symbolist insistence that the arts themselves are concerned primarily with the expression and communication of the state of the artist's soul, i.e. of his subjective emotions. Orage apart, most of the critics discussed or touched upon in this study appear to be in tacit agreement upon this matter, and would probably subscribe to the following account of the way in which the arts generally are supposed to operate: the soul of the artist experiences emotions; these produce physical feelings which the artist embodies in a material work of art. By a reverse process, the soul of the reader or spectator of the work of art is enabled to experience emotions identical with those of the artist. The work of art, in other words, is a type of physical receiver-transmitter which incarnates the artist's experiences on the cosmic plane and allows them to be re-experienced by the less privileged. In *The New Spirit* Havelock Ellis characteristically takes it for granted that what art communicates is the emotion of the artist, and that this communication takes place by a kind of osmosis: 'It is not necessary', he writes, '. . . to distinguish between the emotion of the artist and that of him who merely follows the artist, passing his hand as it were over the other's work, and receiving . . . the same emotion.'[22]

It is sometimes thought that the imagist poets rejected the subjective emotionalism of their predecessors and proposed instead that poetry should devote itself to the exact and objective description of external reality. This is not the case. Pound's criticism is dominated by the view that the sole function of the arts is to express the subjective emotions of the artist. Poetry, he tells us in *The Spirit of Romance,* is 'a sort of inspired mathematics which gives us . . . equations for the human emotions',[23] a position which is maintained throughout his *Gaudier-Brzeska.* His celebrated definition of the Image, which obscures his essentially subjectivist view of poetry, needs to be completed as follows: 'An "Image" is that which presents *to the soul of the reader* an intellectual and emotional complex *in the soul of the poet* in an instant of time.'[24] Pound's 'intellectual and emotional complex' is in fact the poet's mood, or state of mind or soul, and the imagist poem a means of evoking exactly this mood in the reader.

Pound's imagist colleagues do not advocate objective description of the external world for its own sake any more than he does; when they spoke of creating new rhythms, after all, it was for the purpose of expressing 'new moods'. Although Richard Aldington talks about 'Direct treatment of the subject' he soon makes it clear that 'direct treatment' means 'non-descriptive evocation' of the subject, and that the subject itself is the poet's mood. 'We convey an emotion', he says, 'by presenting the object and circumstances of that emotion without comment.'[25] Completing one of T. E. Hulme's key sentences as we did Pound's, we arrive at the following: 'Say the poet is moved by a certain landscape, he selects from that certain images which . . . serve to suggest and evoke *in the mind or soul of the reader* the state he feels.'[26] Or, as Arthur Symons had written in his *Introduction to the Study of Browning* more than twenty years previously: 'The picture calls up the mood.' In his essay on

Whistler of 1903-06 Symons summed up this central aspiration of the modernist and proto-modernist poetic in a single word: 'telepathy'.[27]

That the ideas of Pound and Hulme should have so much in common with those of Symons is not surprising. Most supporters of 'pure poetry' regard it as communicating one of only two things: either the poet's own emotions, or transcendental realities.[28] Symons began by subscribing to the first view, which he called 'impressionism', and later shifted his allegiance to the second, which he called 'symbolism'. Like Yeats he sometimes attempts to have the best of both worlds by ingeniously claiming that the moods of the poet have transcendental status. In his essay on Verlaine in *The Symbolist Movement in Literature,* for example, he claims that the succession of our moods constitutes the more intimate part of our *spiritual* life.

Whatever they may call themselves, Pound, Hulme and Symons, together with a significant number of late-nineteenth-century and early-twentieth-century poets and critics are basically emotional-expressionists. They take the view, which appears to be implicit in T. S. Eliot's doctrine of the 'objective correlative' and was formulated with unusual and commendable clarity by A. E. Housman, that 'To transfuse emotion—not to transmit thought but to set up in the reader's sense a vibration corresponding to what was felt by the writer—is the peculiar function of poetry.'[29] It seems reasonable to infer that emotional-expressionist views of this kind, which are Romantic in origin, became increasingly extreme during the course of the nineteenth century mainly as a consequence of the continual and highly impressive advances which were being made in the natural sciences. The more did scientists come to be regarded as possessing a monopoly in the field of fact and objective truth, the more did artists come to be regarded as dealing solely in their alleged opposites, i.e. subjective visions and emotions. Rejecting naturalism and impressionism on the grounds that these were scientifically inspired, the late-nineteenth-century symbolists and early-twentieth-century expressionists erected this division of territory into a principle and propounded doctrinaire forms of emotional-expressionism which have had the most important practical consequences for subsequent poetry and painting.

By concerning itself purely with the expression of transient and subjective emotions, poetry has become for the most part synonymous with lyric poetry. Other genres of poetry have virtually disappeared: there are few long poems, few narrative poems, few didactic or doctrinal poems, and few humorous, satirical or occasional poems. Indeed, the symbolist assumption that poetry proper is solely concerned with the communication of the poet's *état d'âme* has become so deeply entrenched that many contemporaries would probably still argue that such forms cannot be poetry at all and are necessarily 'verse', which is something qualitatively different. 'Light verse, poor girl, is under a sad weather' still, and 'treated as démodé altogether', just as she was when Auden wrote his 'Letter to Lord Byron' in 1937.

In the field of painting the visionary, transcendental element in symbolism has remained more overtly influential than it has in poetry, so that the consequences have been rather different. They have been no less drastically limiting, however. As a consequence of symbolist anti-realism, *genre* painting, narrative painting and didactic painting are virtually extinct. Twentieth-century *avant-garde* painting has turned its back upon the daily life of the twentieth century so resolutely, and rejected the world of appearances so wholeheartedly, as to imply a basic disparagement of everyday human life in favour of the purely other-worldly. 'The visible world is no longer a reality', as Symons predicted.

The practical effects which I have described are the consequence of certain assumptions, which in their turn derive from certain theoretical premises. The theories themselves have probably by now been largely forgotten, but will need to be re-examined if it is thought necessary to question the assumptions and free poetry and painting from the restrictions which I have outlined. Furthermore, if I am correct in my general estimate of the extent to which twentieth-century modernism is indebted to late-nineteenth-century symbolism, important questions of an intentionalist kind are raised in connection with our interpretation of early-twentieth-century poetry and painting themselves. Assuming for example that Pound's well-known short poem 'In a Station of the Metro' is intended not primarily to describe a scene but to duplicate in the reader's soul Pound's exact emotional mood of a moment long ago, and that Mondrian's austerely geometrical paintings are intended as direct revelations of the nature of the occult world, what are to be our attitudes towards these works?

Should we wish to decide whether or not symbolism's largest and most essential claim is allowable, the issue seems to be put with sufficient clarity in the distinction which Arthur Symons made in his essay on Wordsworth between 'what is preached from the pulpit' and 'what is sung or prayed before the altar'. None of us would presumably wish to deny that poets and painters can be preachers, or that art and literature can be the medium of religious doctrines as in Milton's *Paradise Lost* or the paintings of Duccio. Do we wish however to believe with Symons and Orage that poets and painters are priests, that art and literature are themselves 'a kind of religion', and that a poem or a painting is a 'sacred ritual' capable of mediating occult forces in the manner of a sacrament? Whatever our answer, I do not think it can be denied that as far as poetry and painting are concerned, the symbolist movement has proved to be not a movement of liberation, as Symons hoped, but the means to a new and severer kind of bondage. There have been, as Symons himself said about the poetry of Mallarmé, 'marvellous discoveries by the way', but these appear to have been achieved at far too high a cost.

References

CHAPTER 1

1. Edward Carpenter, *My Days and Dreams. Being Autobiographical Notes* (London, George Allen & Unwin, 1916), p. 240.
2. Bertrand Russell, *Our Knowledge of the External World as a Field for Scientific Method in Philosophy* (Chicago & London, The Open Court Publishing Co., 1914), p. 11.
3. I. F. Clarke, *Voices Prophesying War 1763-1984* (Oxford, Oxford University Press, 1966), Chs III & IV.
4. Robert Schmutzler, *Art Nouveau,* trans. Edouard Roditi (London, Thames & Hudson, 1964), p. 272.
5. *Ibid.* p. 260.
6. M. H. Abrams: *The Mirror and the Lamp: Romantic Theory and the Critical Tradition* (New York, Oxford University Press, 1953), p. 204.
7. Herbert Spencer, *First Principles* (London, Williams & Norgate, 1862), p. 174.
8. Edward Carpenter, 'The Divine Mind and Other Minds', Carpenter Collection, Sheffield Central Library, ms. no. 4, p. 12.
9. Charles Gore (ed.), *Lux Mundi: A Series of Studies in the Religion of the Incarnation* (London, John Murray, 1889), p. 100.
10. *The New Age* (hereafter *N.A.*) XVII, 6 (10 June 1915), pp. 133-4.
11. *N.A.* XVIII, 5 (2 Dec. 1915), p. 110.
12. William K. Wimsatt, Jr. & Cleanth Brooks, *Literary Criticism: A Short History* (New York, Knopf, 1957), p. 370.
13. David Friedrich Strauss, *The Old Faith and the New: A Confession,* trans. Mathilde Blind (London, Asher, 1873), pp. 435-6.
14. Havelock Ellis, *The Dance of Life* (London, Constable, 1923), pp. 198-9.
15. *Ibid.* pp. 200-1.
16. Alasdair MacIntyre (ed.), *Metaphysical Beliefs* (London, S.C.M. Press, 1957), p. 73.

17. Benjamin Kidd, *Social Evolution* (London, Macmillan, 1894), p. 16.
18. G. R. S. Mead (ed.), *Select Works of Plotinus* (London, Bohn, 1895), p. vii.
19. Arthur Symons, *The Symbolist Movement in Literature* (London, Heinemann, 1899), pp. 31-2.
20. *Ibid.* p. 146.
21. Elie Halévy, *A History of the English People: Epilogue, Vol. I, 1895-1905*, trans. E. I. Watkin (London, Benn, 1929), p. 185.
22. Frank Podmore, *Modern Spiritualism: A History and a Criticism* (London, Methuen, 1902), Vol. II, p. 47.
23. *Proceedings of the Society for Psychical Research* I (1882-3), p. 3.
24. Alan Willard Brown, *The Metaphysical Society: Victorian Minds in Crisis, 1869-1880* (New York, Columbia University Press, 1947), p. 279.
25. Laurence Oliphant, *Fashionable Philosophy and Other Sketches* (Edinburgh & London, Blackwood, 1887), p. 12. 'Fashionable Philosophy' first appeared in *Blackwood's Magazine* for May 1884, and 'The Sisters of Tibet' in *The Nineteenth Century* for November 1884.
26. Edmund Garrett, *Isis Very Much Unveiled, Being the Story of the Great Mahatma Hoax* (London, *Westminster Gazette* Office, [1895]), p. 16.
27. *Proceedings of the Society for Psychical Research* III (1885), p. 207.
28. Philip Mairet, *A. R. Orage: A Memoir* (London, Dent, 1936), p. 16.
29. A. P. Sinnett, *The Occult World* (London, Trübner, 1881), p. 6.
30. A. P. Sinnett, *Esoteric Buddhism* (London, Trübner, 1883), p. 197.
31. *Ibid.* p. 29.
32. Cf. S. B. Liljegren, 'Bulwer-Lytton's Novels and Isis Unveiled', *Upsala University English Institute Essays and Studies on English Language and Literature* XVIII.
33. C. Nelson Stewart, *Bulwer Lytton as an Occultist* (London, The Theosophical Publishing House, 1927), pp. 1-2.
34. Richard Le Gallienne, *The Book-Bills of Narcissus: An Account Rendered by R. Le Gallienne* (Derby, Leicester & Nottingham, Frank Murray, 1891), p. 30.
35. W. B. Yeats, *Ideas of Good and Evil* (London, A. H. Bullen, 1903), p. 29.

36. Bulwer Lytton, *A Strange Story* (London, Sampson Low, 1862), p. 86.
37. See Joseph I. Fradin, ' "The Absorbing Tyranny of Every-Day Life": Bulwer Lytton's *A Strange Story*', *Nineteenth-Century Fiction* XVI, 1 (June 1961), pp. 15-16.
38. A. G. Lehmann, *The Symbolist Aesthetic in France 1885-1895* (Oxford, Blackwell, 1950), pp. 55-67.
39. Franz Hueffer, *Richard Wagner and the Music of the Future: History and Aesthetics* (London, Chapman & Hall, 1874), pp. 9-10.
40. Edward Carpenter, *The Art of Creation: Essays on the Self and Its Powers* (London, George Allen, 1904) pp. vii-viii.
41. Bernard Bosanquet, *The Philosophical Theory of the State* (London, Macmillan, 1899), p. 152.
42. H. G. Wells, *Anticipations of the Reactions of Mechanical and Scientific Progress Upon Human Life and Thought* (London, Chapman & Hall, 1902), p. 246.
43. Oscar Wilde, 'The Soul of Man Under Socialism', *The Fortnightly Review* XLIX, CCXC n.s. (Feb. 1891), p. 316.
44. Francis Galton, *Inquiries into Human Faculty and Its Development* (London, Macmillan, 1883), p. 24 n.
45. *Ibid.* p. 304.
46. Havelock Ellis, *The Task of Social Hygiene* (London, Constable, 1913), p. 402.
47. *N.A.* VII, 11 (14 July 1910), p. 261.
48. J. M. Kennedy, *Tory Democracy* (London, Stephen Swift, 1911), p. 202.
49. J. M. Kennedy, *English Literature 1880-1905* (London, Stephen Swift, 1912), p. 248.
50. C. P. Snow, *The Two Cultures and the Scientific Revolution* (Cambridge, Cambridge University Press, 1960), p. 7.
51. Arthur J. Marder, *British Naval Policy 1880-1905: The Anatomy of British Sea Power* (London, Putnam, 1941), p. 20.
52. *Ibid.* p. 18.
53. Havelock Ellis, *Views and Reviews: A Selection of Uncollected Articles 1884-1932. First Series: 1884-1919* (London, Harmsworth, 1932), p. 52.
54. Friedrich Nietzsche, *Thoughts Out of Season*, trans. Ludovici (Edinburgh & London, T. N. Foulis, 1909), Part 1, p. 8.
55. Friedrich Nietzsche, *The Case of Wagner; Nietzsche contra Wagner; The Twilight of the Idols; The Antichrist*, trans. Common (London, Henry, 1896), p. 25.
56. *N.A.* XIV, 2 (13 Nov. 1913), p. 51.
57. *N.A.* XIV, 4 (27 Nov. 1913), p. 113.

58. T. E. Hulme (ed. S. Hynes), *Further Speculations* (Minneapolis, University of Minnesota Press, 1955), p. xxxi.
59. *N.A.* IV, 11 (7 Jan. 1909), p. 225.
60. *English Literature 1880-1905,* p. 25.
61. *Ibid.* p. 78.
62. 'The Social Organism' was originally published in *The Westminster Review* for January 1860.
63. E. Ray Lankester, *Degeneration: A Chapter in Darwinism* (London, Macmillan, 1880), p. 61.
64. Havelock Ellis, *The Problem of Race-Regeneration* (London, Cassell, 1911), p. 7.
65. Cesare Lombroso, *The Man of Genius,* trans. Ellis (London, Walter Scott, 1891), p. vi.
66. J. F. Nisbet, *The Insanity of Genius* (London, Ward & Downey, 1891), p. xv.
67. Francis Galton, *Hereditary Genius. An Inquiry into Its Laws and Consequences* (London, Macmillan, 1892), p. ix.
68. Havelock Ellis, *The Criminal* (London, Walter Scott, 1890), p. 139.
69. *Ibid.* p. 187.
70. *The Man of Genius,* p. 238.
71. *Ibid.* p. 359.
72. Max Nordau, *Degeneration* (London, Heinemann, 1895), p. viii.
73. *Punch, Or the London Charivari,* 108, 2806 (20 April 1895), p. 183.
74. E. Purcell, 'Max Nordau's "Degeneration"', *The Academy,* no. 1205 (8 June 1895), p. 475.
75. *Degeneration,* p. 416.

CHAPTER 2

1. Houston Peterson, *Havelock Ellis: Philosopher of Love* (Boston & New York, Houghton Mifflin, 1928), pp. 383-6.
2. *Views and Reviews: First Series,* pp. 3-4.
3. *Ibid.* p. 47.
4. *The New Spirit* (London, Bell, 1890), p. 5.
5. *Ibid.* pp. 244-5.
6. *Affirmations* (London, Walter Scott, 1898), p. 210.
7. 'Science and Mysticism', *The Atlantic Monthly* CXI (June 1913), p. 783; *The Dance of Life* (London, Constable, 1923), p. 213.

8. *The Dance of Life,* pp. x-xi.
9. *Views and Reviews: First Series,* p. 37.
10. *The New Spirit,* p. v.
11. *The New Spirit* (fourth edition: London, Constable, 1926), p. viii.
12. *The New Spirit,* p. 137.
13. *The Dance of Life,* p. 149.
14. *Affirmations,* p. 160.
15. *Imaginary Conversations by Walter Savage Landor* (London, Walter Scott, 1886), p. xvi.
16. *The New Spirit,* p. 6.
17. *My Life* (London, Heinemann, 1940), p. 41.
18. 'A Mad Saint', *The Savoy* II (April 1896), p. 21.
19. *Views and Reviews: First Series,* pp. 150-1.
20. *Ibid.* p. 309.
21. *Ibid.* p. 84.
22. 'The Celtic Spirit in Literature', *The Contemporary Review* LXXXIX (Feb. 1906), p. 217.
23. 'The Colour-Sense in Literature', *The Contemporary Review* LXIX (May 1896), p. 729.
24. *Vasari's Lives of Italian Painters* (London, Walter Scott, 1895), p. xiii.
25. *Affirmations,* pp. 116-17.
26. *Ibid.* pp. 138, 141.
27. *Imaginary Conversations,* p. xix.
28. *Views and Reviews: First Series,* p. 35.
29. *Ibid.* p. 42.
30. *The Prose Writings of Heinrich Heine* (London, Walter Scott, 1887), p. 148.
31. *Views and Reviews: First Series,* p. 50.
32. *The New Spirit,* p. 32.
33. *Ibid.* p. 157.
34. *Ibid.* pp. 105-6.
35. *Ibid.* p. 112.
36. *Ibid.* pp. 123-4.
37. *Affirmations,* pp. 16-17.
38. *Ibid.* p. 187.
39. *Ibid.* pp. 186-7.
40. *Ibid.* p. 206.
41. *Ibid.* p. 211.
42. *Views and Reviews: First Series,* p. 59.
43. *Ibid.* p. 60.
44. 'The Novels of Thomas Hardy', *The Westminster Review* CXIX, LXIII n.s. (April 1883), p. 358.

45. 'Concerning Jude the Obscure', *The Savoy* VI (Oct. 1896), p. 35.
46. *Affirmations,* pp. 151-2.
47. *Ibid.* p. 148.
48. *Degeneration,* pp. 499, 500.
49. *Affirmations,* p. 242.
50. *Ibid.* p. 125.
51. *The Nineteenth Century: A Dialogue in Utopia* (London, Grant Richards, 1900), pp. 66-7.
52. *Ibid.* pp. 94-5.
53. *Ibid.* pp. 81-2.
54. *The New Spirit,* p. v.
55. Holbrook Jackson, *The Eighteen Nineties* (London, Grant Richards, 1913), pp. 20-2.
56. *The New Spirit,* p. 9.

CHAPTER 3

1. 'Paul Verlaine', *The National and English Review* 19 (June 1892), p. 506.
2. 'The Decadent Movement in Literature', *Harper's New Monthly Magazine* (American edition) LXXXVII (Nov. 1893), p. 866.
3. '*Bonheur.* Par Paul Verlaine', *The Academy* XXXIX, 989 n.s. (18 April 1891), p. 362. See also note 17 below.
4. 'J. K. Huysmans', *The Fortnightly Review* LI n.s. (March 1892), p. 413.
5. *The Savoy* VIII (Dec. 1896), p. 93.
6. 'A Symbolist Farce', *The Saturday Review* 82, 2147 (19 Dec. 1896), p. 646.
7. 'A Note on George Meredith', *The Fortnightly Review* LXII n.s. (Nov. 1897), p. 677.
8. 'Aubrey Beardsley', *The Fortnightly Review* LXIII n.s. (May 1898), p. 756.
9. *The Symbolist Movement in Literature,* ed. *cit.* p. 8.
10. *An Introduction to the Study of Browning* (London, Cassell, 1886), p. 23.
11. *Ibid.* p. 24.
12. 'Browning's Last Poems', *The Academy* XXXVII, 923 n.s. (11 Jan. 1890), p. 19.
13. 'Frederi Mistral', *The National Review* 35 (Jan. 1886), p. 660.

14. *Impressions and Opinions. By George Moore*, *The Academy* XXXIX, 985 n.s. (21 March 1891), p. 274.
15. 'Paul Verlaine', *loc. cit.* p. 515.
16. 'Mr. Henley's Poetry', *The Fortnightly Review* LII n.s. (Aug. 1892), p. 186.
17. *Ibid.* p. 192.
18. 'The Decadent Movement in Literature', *loc. cit.*, p. 859.
19. *Ibid.* p. 860.
20. 'Robert Browning and George Meredith', *Papers of the Browning Society. Volume 2. London 1885-89* (Nendeln, Kraus Reprint, 1966), p. 81*.
21. *Time* XIV (Feb. 1886), p. 247.
22. 'Paul Verlaine', *Black and White* I, 20 (20 June 1891), p. 649.
23. *Silhouettes* (London, Mathews & Lane, 1892), p. 81.
24. *'Religio Poetae,* &c. By Coventry Patmore', *The Athenaeum* 3453 (30 Dec. 1893), pp. 902-3.
25. 'Christina Rossetti', *The Saturday Review* 79, 2045 (5 Jan. 1895), pp. 5-6.
26. 'M. Huysmans as Mystic', *The Saturday Review* 79, 2054 (9 March 1895), p. 313.
27. 'Coventry Patmore', *The New Review* 16 (1896-97), p. 74.
28. 'Maeterlinck as a Mystic', *The Contemporary Review* LXXII (Sept. 1897), p. 351.
29. *The Symbolist Movement in Literature,* pp. 5-6.
30. *Ibid.* p. 32.
31. 'Rodin', *The Fortnightly Review* LXXI n.s. (June 1902), p. 967.
32. 'Eleonora Duse', *The Contemporary Review* LXXVIII (Aug. 1900), pp. 201-2.
33. Gabriele D'Annunzio, *The Child of Pleasure,* trans. Georgina Harding (London, Heinemann, 1898), p. ix.
34. *The Symbolist Movement in Literature* (London, Constable, 1908), pp. 143-4.
35. 'Balzac', *The Fortnightly Review* LXV n.s. (May 1899), pp. 745-57.
36. 'Ballet, Pantomime, and Poetic Drama', *The Dome* VI n.s. (Oct. 1898), pp. 65-71.
37. *Plays Acting and Music. A Book of Theory* (London, Constable, 1909), pp. 211-12.
38. *Ibid.* p. 311.
39. 'Henrik Ibsen', *The Quarterly Review* 205, 409 (Oct. 1906), p. 396.

40. 'D'Annunzio's "Francesca da Rimini" ', *The Fortnightly Review* LXXI n.s. (Feb. 1902), p. 246.
41. 'A New Art of the Stage', *The Monthly Review* VII, 3 (June 1902), p. 162.
42. 'An Apology for Puppets', *The Saturday Review* 84, 2177 (17 July 1897), p. 56.
43. 'Ballet, Pantomime, and Poetic Drama', *loc. cit.* p. 70.
44. 'The Price of Realism', *The Academy and Literature* LXIII, 1581 (23 Aug. 1902), p. 200.
45. 'A New Art of the Stage', *loc. cit.* p. 157.
46. *The Symbolist Movement in Literature*, pp. 107-8.
47. 'The Ballad of Reading Gaol', *The Saturday Review* 85, 2211 (12 March 1898), p. 365.
48. 'Robert Bridges', *The Monthly Review* IV, 1 (July 1901), p. 126.
49. 'Mr. Yeats as a Lyric Poet', *The Saturday Review* 87, 2271 (6 May 1899), p. 553.
50. 'John Keats', *The Monthly Review* V, 1 (Oct. 1901), p. 155.
51. 'The Poetry of Landor', *The Atlantic Monthly* LXXXIX (June 1906), p. 813.
52. 'Mr. Leslie Stephen as a Critic', *The Saturday Review* 86, 2230 (23 July 1898), p. 113.
53. 'Campoamor. The Great Spanish Poet of the Nineteenth Century,' *Harper's New Monthly Magazine* CIV (Dec. 1901), p. 128.
54. 'St. Teresa and St. John of the Cross', *The Contemporary Review* LXXV (April 1899), p. 547.
55. *Studies in Two Literatures* (London, Smithers, 1897), p. 143.
56. 'Wordsworth', *The Fortnightly Review* LXXI n.s. (Jan. 1902), p. 41.
57. 'Ballet, Pantomime, and Poetic Drama', *loc. cit.* p. 67.
58. *The Symbolist Movement in Literature*, p. 106.
59. *Ibid.* pp. 131-2.
60. 'Ballet, Pantomime, and Poetic Drama', *loc. cit.* p. 67.
61. 'Mr. Yeats as a Lyric Poet', *loc. cit.* p. 553.
62. Emile Verhaeren, *The Dawn*, trans. Symons (London, Duckworth, 1898), p. 7.
63. 'Rodin', *loc. cit.* p. 960.
64. 'Is Browning Dramatic?' Read for Symons by Dr. Furnivall on 30 January 1885. (Paper XXVIII, p. 1, in *Papers of the Browning Society 1885-89*.)
65. 'The Lesson of Millais', *The Savoy* VI (Oct. 1896), p. 57.

66. 'Tolstoi on Art. II', *The Saturday Review* 86, 2232 (6 Aug. 1898), p. 180.
67. 'A New Guide to Journalism', *The Saturday Review* 96, 2493 (8 Aug. 1903), p. 165.
68. 'The Art of Watts', *The Fortnightly Review* LXVIII n.s. (Aug. 1900), p. 195.
69. 'Monna Vanna', *The Academy and Literature* LXIII, 1574 (5 July 1902), p. 45.
70. 'Henry de Groux', *The Art Journal,* July 1904, p. 232; 'Gustave Moreau', *The Monthly Review* XX, 1 (July 1905), pp. 125-6, 128-30.
71. *Plays Acting and Music, ed. cit.* p. 257.
72. 'Balzac', *loc. cit.* p. 754.
73. 'Henrik Ibsen', *loc. cit.* p. 395.
74. *William Blake* (London, Constable, 1907), p. 82.
75. *The Fool of the World & Other Poems* (London, Heinemann, 1906), pp. 13-14. I have substituted a comma for the incorrect full-stop after 'strife'.
76. 'A Book of Songs', *The Nation* I, 17 (22 June 1907), p. 639.
77. *The Symbolist Movement in Literature,* p. 174.
78. 'Modern Caricature and Impressionism', *Blast. Review of the Great English Vortex* 2 (July 1915), p. 79.
79. 'Aubrey Beardsley', *loc. cit.* p. 760.
80. W. B. Yeats, *Autobiographies* (London, Macmillan, 1955), pp. 319-21.
81. *The Criterion* IX, 35 (Jan. 1930), p. 357.
82. G. Thomas Tanselle, 'Two Early Letters of Ezra Pound', *American Literature* XXXIV, 1 (March 1962), p. 118.
83. Ezra Pound, 'The Later Yeats', *Poetry* IV, 11 (May 1914), p. 68.
84. As for note 82 above.
85. A. C. Bradley, 'Poetry for Poetry's Sake', *Oxford Lectures on Poetry* (London, Macmillan, 1909), pp. 3-27.
86. Michael Roberts, *T. E. Hulme* (London, Faber & Faber, 1938), p. 265.
87. T. E. Hulme, 'Searchers after Reality. II. Haldane', *N.A.* V, 17 (19 Aug. 1909), p. 315.
88. Ezra Pound, *Make It New* (London, Faber & Faber, 1934), p. 361.
89. Stanley K. Coffman, Jr, *Imagism. A Chapter for the History of Modern Poetry* (Norman, University of Oklahoma, 1951), p. 28.

CHAPTER 4

1. D. D. Paige (ed.), *The Letters of Ezra Pound: 1907-1941* (New York, Harcourt Brace, 1950), p. 259.
2. *N.A.* XXXVIII, 20 (18 March 1926), p. 235.
3. *The Labour Leader* VII, 86 n.s. (30 Nov. 1895), p. 3. I have silently corrected minor printing errors in quotations from this periodical.
4. *Ibid.* VIII, 106 n.s. (11 April 1896), p. 122.
5. *Ibid.* VIII, 105 n.s. (4 April 1896), p. 114.
6. *Ibid.* VIII, 132 n.s. (10 Oct. 1896), p. 352.
7. *Ibid.* VIII, 103 n.s. (21 March 1896), p. 102; VIII, 121 n.s. (25 July 1896), p. 258.
8. *Ibid.* VIII, 127 n.s. (5 Sept. 1896), p. 308.
9. *Ibid.* VIII, 114 n.s. (6 June 1896), p. 197.
10. *Ibid.* VIII, 117 n.s. (27 June 1896), p. 218.
11. *The Symbolist Movement in Literature,* p. 146.
12. *The Labour Leader* VIII, 114 n.s. (6 June 1896), p. 197.
13. Holbrook Jackson, *Bernard Shaw: a Monograph* (London, Grant Richards, 1907), pp. 11-12.
14. A. R. Orage, *Friedrich Nietzsche: The Dionysian Spirit of the Age* (London & Edinburgh, T. N. Foulis, 1906), pp. 74-5.
15. *N.A.* XVI, 2 (12 Nov. 1914), p. 42.
16. Arthur Symons, *William Blake,* pp. 1-2.
17. W. B. Yeats, *Ideas of Good and Evil,* p. 201.
18. *Friedrich Nietzsche,* p. 12.
19. 'Readings and Re-Readings: "Zanoni" ', *The Theosophical Review* XXXI, 184 (15 Dec. 1902), p. 344.
20. *Nietzsche in Outline and Aphorism* (Edinburgh & London, T.N. Foulis, 1907), p. 47.
21. *Friedrich Nietzsche,* p. 75.
22. *Consciousness: Animal, Human, and Superman* (London & Benares, Theosophical Publishing Society, 1907), p. 74.
23. 'Esprit de Corps in Elementary Schools', *The Monthly Review* XXV, 75 (Dec. 1906), p. 50. ('Discipline in Elementary Schools' appeared in *The Monthly Review* for May 1907.)
24. 'Politics for Craftsmen', *The Contemporary Review* XCI (June 1907), p. 785.
25. *N.A.* I, 23 (23 Oct. 1907), p. 362.
26. *N.A.* II, 1 (31 Oct. 1907), p. 10.
27. 'The New Romanticism', *The Theosophical Review* XL, 235 (March 1907), p. 55.
28. 'Esprit de Corps in Elementary Schools', *loc. cit.* p. 48.
29. *N.A.* II, 4 (21 Nov. 1907), p. 70.

30. *N.A.* II, 3 (14 Nov. 1907), p. 50.
31. *Nietzsche in Outline and Aphorism,* p. 66.
32. 'Readings and Re-Readings: The Mystic Valuation of Literature', *The Theosophical Review* XXXI, 185 (15 Jan. 1903), p. 430.
33. *Consciousness: Animal, Human, and Superman,* p. 83.
34. *Nietzsche in Outline and Aphorism,* p. 124.
35. *Ibid.* pp. 65-6.
36. *Ibid.* p. 61.
37. *N.A.* XXVIII, 3 (18 Nov. 1920), p. 30.
38. *N.A.* IV, 20 (11 March 1909), p. 399.
39. *N.A.* X, 16 (15 Feb. 1912), p. 371.
40. *N.A.* X, 3 (16 Nov. 1911), p. 49.
41. George Dangerfield, *The Strange Death of Liberal England* (London, McGibbon & Kee, 1966), p. 12.
42. *N.A.* XI, 17 (22 Aug. 1912), p. 388.
43. *N.A.* XI, 16 (15 Aug. 1912), pp. 373-4.
44. *N.A.* IX, 22 (28 Sept. 1911), p. 518.
45. *N.A.* XI, 4 (23 May 1912), p. 85.
46. *N.A.* IV, 19 (4 March 1909), p. 379.
47. Frederic Harrison, 'Aischro-Latreia—The Cult of the Foul', *The Nineteenth Century and After* 420 (Feb. 1912), p. 333.
48. Oscar Wilde, *Intentions* (London, Osgood McIlvaine, 1891), p. 22.
49. *N.A.* VIII, 9 (29 Dec. 1910), p. 204.
50. *N.A.* IX, 24 (12 Oct. 1911), p. 563.
51. *Ibid.*
52. *N.A.* IX, 2 (11 May 1911), p. 35.
53. *N.A.* X, 24 (11 April 1912), p. 564.
54. *N.A.* IX, 23 (5 Oct. 1911), p. 539.
55. *N.A.* IX, 24 (12 Oct. 1911), p. 562.
56. *N.A.* X, 16 (15 Feb. 1912), p. 371.
57. *N.A.* XVII, 25 (21 Oct. 1915), p. 597.
58. *N.A.* XVIII, 20 (16 March 1916), p. 470.
59. *N.A.* XIII, 17 (21 Aug. 1913), p. 486.
60. *N.A.* XVII, 6 (10 June 1915), p. 133.
61. *N.A.* XIII, 11 (10 July 1913), p. 297.
62. *N.A.* XVI, 3 (19 Nov. 1914), p. 69.
63. *N.A.* XIII, 13 (24 July 1913), p. 362.
64. *N.A.* XIII, 26 (23 Oct. 1913), p. 761.
65. *N.A.* XIV, 8 (25 Dec. 1913), p. 241.
66. *N.A.* XIII, 22 (25 Sept. 1913), p. 634.
67. A. R. Orage, *Readers and Writers (1917-1921)* (New York, Knopf, 1922), preface.

68. *N.A.* XIII, 27 (30 Oct. 1913), p. 792.
69. *N.A.* XVII, 13 (29 July 1915), p. 309.
70. A. R. Orage, *Selected Essays and Critical Writings,* ed. Herbert Read & Denis Saurat (London, Stanley Nott, 1935), pp. 152-3. The version quoted prints 'caution' for what should clearly be 'emotion'.
71. *N.A.* XVIII, 20 (16 March 1916), p. 470.
72. *N.A.* XVI, 24 (15 April 1915), p. 642.
73. *N.A.* XXI, 12 (19 July 1917), p. 267.
74. *N.A.* XVIII, 4 (25 Nov. 1915), p. 85.
75. *The Symbolist Movement in Literature,* p. 90.
76. A. R. Orage, *The Art of Reading* (New York, Farrar & Rinehart, 1930), p. 73.
77. *N.A.* XVIII, 5 (2 Dec 1915), p. 110.
78. Ezra Pound, 'Vortex', *Blast* 1 (20 June 1914), p. 154.
79. Wyndham Lewis, 'Modern Caricature and Impressionism', *Blast* 2 (July 1915), p. 79.
80. Boris Ford (ed.), *The Pelican Guide to English Literature* (Harmondsworth, Penguin Books, 1961), Vol. 7, pp. 88-9.

CHAPTER 5

1. J. I. M. Stewart, *Eight Modern Writers* (Oxford, Oxford University Press, 1963), p. 312.
2. Havelock Ellis, *The New Spirit,* pp. 234-5.
3. *Ibid.* p. 235.
4. Havelock Ellis, *Affirmations,* p. iii.
5. *Ibid.* p. iv.
6. Wyndham Lewis, *Time and Western Man* (London, Chatto & Windus, 1927), p. 198.
7. Ezra Pound, *Gaudier-Brzeska: A Memoir* (London, Laidlaw & Laidlaw, [1939]), pp. 157, 167.
8. John Heydon, *Theomagia, or The Temple of Wisdome* (London, for Henry Brome and for Tho. Rooks, 1664), Bk I, p. 226.
9. Stuart Gilbert, *James Joyce's 'Ulysses': A Study* (London, Faber & Faber, 1930), p. 52.
10. M. J. C. Hodgart, 'Work in Progress', *The Cambridge Journal* VI, 1 (Oct. 1952), p. 36.
11. F. Max Müller (ed.), *The Sacred Books of the East* (Oxford, Clarendon Press, 1900), Vol. XI, pp. 61-3.

12. T. S. Eliot, *Burnt Norton* (London, Faber & Faber, 1941), p. 11.

13. T. S. Eliot, *The Dry Salvages* (London, Faber & Faber, 1941), p. 14.

14. Ellsworth Mason & Richard Ellman (eds): *The Critical Writings of James Joyce* (London, Faber & Faber, 1959), pp. 221-2.

15. T. H. Gibbons: 'The "Waste Land" Tarot Identified', *Journal of Modern Literature* II (Nov. 1972), pp. 560-5.

16. T. S. Eliot (ed. Valerie Eliot), *The Waste Land; A Facsimile and Transcript of the Original Drafts Including the Annotations of Ezra Pound* (London, Faber & Faber, 1971), p. 37.

17. *Ibid.* p. 31.

18. Sixten Ringbom, 'Art in "The Epoch of the Great Spiritual." Occult Elements in the Early Theory of Abstract Painting', *Journal of the Warburg and Courtauld Institutes* XXIX (1966), pp. 386-418.

19. Martin S. James, 'The Realism Behind Mondrian's Geometry', *Art News* LVI (Dec. 1957), p. 60.

20. Frank Kermode, *Romantic Image* (London, Routledge & Kegan Paul, 1957), pp. 165-6.

21. Cleanth Brooks, *The Well-Wrought Urn* (New York, Reynal & Hitchcock, 1947), Ch. 11.

22. *The New Spirit,* p. 234.

23. Ezra Pound, *The Spirit of Romance* (Norfolk, New Directions, n.d.), p. 14.

24. Ezra Pound, 'A Few Dont's by an Imagiste', *Poetry* I, 6 (March 1913), p. 200.

25. Coffman, *Imagism,* p. 166.

26. Michael Roberts, *T. E. Hulme,* p. 266.

27. Arthur Symons, *Studies in Seven Arts* (London, Constable, 1906), p. 136.

28. Sister Clarice de Sainte Marie Dion: *The Idea of 'Pure Poetry' in English Criticism, 1900-1945* (Washington, D.C., Catholic University of America, 1948), Ch. III.

29. A. E. Housman, *The Name and Nature of Poetry* (Cambridge, Cambridge University Press, 1933), p. 12.

Index

Abercrombie, Lascelles, 116
Abrams, M. H., 4
Academy, The, 37, 67
Addison, Joseph, 47
Adventures of Harry Richmond, The, 75
Agamemnon, The, 83
Aldington, Richard, 99, 141
'Allmash, Mrs', 16
All the Year Round, 20
Also sprach Zarathustra, 26, 106, 110
Arcana Coelestia, 136
A Rebours, 70
Arnold, Sir Edwin, 16, 103
Arnold, Matthew, 33, 66
Arnould, Arthur, 133
Art nouveau, 3-4
Ascidians, 34
Asolando: Facts and Fancies, 71
Athenaeum, The, 68
Auden, W. H., 143
Auschwitz, 28, 29
Axêl, 82, 89

Back to Methuselah, 7
Ballad of Reading Gaol, The, 85
Balzac, Honoré de, 82, 91, 116
Baudelaire, Charles, 30, 70, 90
Beardsley, Aubrey, 70, 95, 126
Bedborough, George, 41
Beethoven, Ludwig van, 22
Belloc, Hilaire, 114
Bennett, Arnold, 120
Bergson, Henri, 2, 3, 11, 89
Berkeley, Bishop George, 23
Besant, Annie, 17, 138
Bhagavad-Gita, 106
Björnson, B. M., 65
Blake, William, 55, 92, 94, 106, 132, 135
BLAST, 2, 95, 121
Blavatsky, Helena Petrova, 1, 16, 17, 19, 108, 132, 133, 134

'Bloom, Leopold', 136
Boehme, Jacob, 42, 79
Bosanquet, Bernard, 12, 25
Bouguereau, W. A., 55
Bourget, Paul, 30-1, 33, 52, 54, 57, 59, 65, 122, 124
Bradley, A. C., 96
Bradley, F. H., 12
Brandes, Georg, 65
Breuer, Josef, 41
Bridges, Robert, 85
British Museum Subject Index, 1881-1900, The, 10
Broca, Paul, 48
Brooks, Cleanth, 138
Brown, Alan Willard, 16
Brown, Catherine, 22
Brown, Ford Madox, 22
Browning, Robert, 14, 49, 71, 90, 96
Browning Society Papers, 67
Büchner, Ludwig, 129
Buddha, 23
Buddha's Fire Sermon, The, 134
Buddhism, Esoteric, 16, 18, 19
Butchart, Montgomery, 101

Caird, Edward, 12
Calendar of Modern Letters, The, 126
Campoamor, Ramon de, 86, 96
Carlyle, Thomas, 28, 102, 129
Carpenter, Edward, 1, 5, 23, 43, 44, 52, 53, 101, 103, 104, 110
Casanova de Seingalt, Giacomo, 50, 56
Cavalcanti, Guido, 97
Chamber Music, 94
Chandler, Alice, 27
Chaucer, Geoffrey, 50, 60
Chesterton, Cecil, 24, 27
Chesterton, G. K., 27, 121
Christian Mysticism, 13
Christ, Jesus, 23, 44